Modern America

1964–Present

DISCOVERING U.S. HISTORY

The New World: Prehistory–1542

Colonial America: 1543–1763

Revolutionary America: 1764–1789

Early National America: 1790–1850

The Civil War Era: 1851–1865

The New South and the Old West: 1866–1890

The Gilded Age and Progressivism: 1891–1913

World War I and the Roaring Twenties: 1914–1928

The Great Depression: 1929–1938

World War II: 1939–1945

The Cold War and Postwar America: 1946–1963

Modern America: 1964–Present

DISCOVERING U.S. HISTORY

Modern America
1964–Present

Tim McNeese

Consulting Editor: Richard Jensen, Ph.D.

CHELSEA HOUSE
PUBLISHERS
An imprint of Infobase Publishing

MODERN AMERICA: 1964–Present

Chelsea House
An imprint of Infobase Publishing
132 West 31st Street
New York NY 10001

Library of Congress Cataloging-in-Publication Data
McNeese, Tim.
  Modern America : 1964-present / by Tim McNeese.
      p. cm. -- (Discovering U.S. History)
  Includes bibliographical references and index.
  ISBN 978-1-60413-361-5 (hardcover : alk. paper) 1. United
States—Politics and government—1945–1989—Juvenile literature.
2. United States—Politics and government—1989—Juvenile literature.
3. Presidents—United States—History—20th century—Juvenile literature.
4. Presidents—United States—History—21st century--Juvenile literature.
I. Title. II. Series.

  E839.5.M359 2009
  973.92--dc22
                              2009048576

The Discovering U.S. History series was produced for Chelsea House by
Bender Richardson White, Uxbridge, UK

Editors: Lionel Bender and Susan Malyan
Designer and Picture Researcher: Ben White
Production: Kim Richardson
Maps and graphics: Stefan Chabluk
Cover design: Alicia Post

Cover printed by Bang Printing, Brainerd, MN
Book printed and bound by Bang Printing, Brainerd, MN
Date printed: April 2010
Printed in the United States of America

This book is printed on acid-free paper.

Contents

Introduction
Creating a New Society

He would not be the first U.S. president to deliver a speech in the shadow of Berlin's Brandenburg Gate, but he wanted his words to ring with intent and purpose. The year was 1987. Ronald Reagan would be speaking within sight of one the most politically potent symbols of the Communist world—the Berlin Wall. He wanted to use the Wall to make a case against the Soviet Union, which he had referred to as an "evil empire."

At 76 years of age, President Reagan was old enough to have heard adults in 1917 discussing how revolutionaries had overthrown the last of the Russian czars, Nicholas II. Throughout Reagan's entire lifetime, Communism had not only dominated Russia and the Soviet states, but its adherents had worked to spread its influence around the world, including to Berlin at the very heart of Europe. One theme had run consistently through Ronald Reagan's life—his bitter hatred of Communism.

A DIVIDING WALL

Reagan could easily remember when the Berlin Wall had become reality. The Soviets had erected it in August 1961, when their Premier, Nikita Khrushchev, had finally tired of the drain of German citizens from East Berlin, which had been under Soviet control since the years immediately following the end of World War II (1945). Leaving Communist-controlled East Berlin had been as simple as boarding a subway or surface train and taking a ride to the freedoms found in West Berlin. As one East Berliner remembered, notes historian John Gaddis, "You could go from socialism… to capitalism in two minutes."

By 1961, 2.7 million Germans had left the misery and oppression of the East, opting for greater opportunities in the West. But Khrushchev had finally had enough. His answer was to order the construction of a wall, patrolled by border guards with orders to shoot-to-kill anyone who tried to leave East Berlin. That would keep them in, the determined Soviet leader had thought. In 1963 President John F. Kennedy made a trip to Europe that included a symbolic visit to the Berlin Wall. When the president stood at the Wall, within earshot of those on the other side, the speech he intended to provide hope was spoken in anger:

> *There are many people in the world who really don't understand, or say they don't, what is the great issue between the free world and the Communist world. Let them come to Berlin. There are some who say that Communism is the wave of the future. Let them come to Berlin. And there are some who say, in Europe and elsewhere, we can work with the Communists. Let them come to Berlin. And there are even a few who say that it is true that Communism is an evil system, but it permits us to make economic progress. Lass' sie nach Berlin kommen.* Let them come to Berlin.

This speech brought cheers from the great throng of West Berliners, even as East German border guards pushed East Berliners away from their side of the Wall so they could not hear the president's words.

A NEW BERLIN SPEECH

Despite Kennedy's speech, the Berlin Wall remained. Twenty-four years passed and a half-dozen U.S. presidents took office. Each had met the challenges of Soviet Communism in his own way. From the end of World War II the leaders of the United States had engaged in a prolonged conflict known as the Cold War, which pitted the political will of the Communist East against the freedom-loving West. They had gone to war in Korea and in Vietnam to push back the advance of Communism. They had encouraged Congress to send support to those nations threatened by Communist takeover. Presidents had negotiated nuclear arms agreements and engaged in cordial dialogue. They supported freedom fighters bent on turning back the challenge of Marxism. But Communism had continued, the Soviets had remained a powerful force against the United States, and the Berlin Wall still stood. Now another U.S. president was preparing to give another speech against the backdrop of the Berlin Wall.

Words Meant to Challenge

When the day came for Reagan to deliver his speech, he, like Kennedy, was moved to anger. He too watched as police on the East Berlin side tried to herd people away from the Wall. But before him were thousands of West Berliners, ready to hear the president speak, just as an earlier generation had gathered to listen to Kennedy. As he opened his speech, Reagan too included a little German, as JFK had done: "I join your fellow countrymen in the West, in this firm, this unalterable belief: *Es gibt nur ein Berlin.*" ("There is only one

On June 12, 1987, President Ronald Reagan stood before the Berlin Wall and challenged Soviet leader Mikhail Gorbachev to tear down the wall.

Berlin.") Reagan then launched into his full address, recounting the days of 1945 when the war in Europe had finally ended. He remembered how the Soviets had taken over in the East and had divided the city so many decades ago. He recalled the recovery of West Germany and the prosperity and stability the people of West Berlin had experienced since the war. Then, he came to a line that would resonate more than he could have imagined. Sternly, he spoke:

> *There is one sign the Soviets can make that would be unmistakable, that would advance dramatically the cause of freedom and peace. General Secretary Gorbachev, if you seek peace, if you seek prosperity for the Soviet Union and Eastern Europe, if you seek liberalization, come here to this gate! Mr. Gorbachev, open this gate. Mr. Gorbachev, tear down this wall!*

The crowd applauded and cheered enthusiastically. Perhaps as Reagan spoke that day in 1987, he said more than he knew. He could not have known that his words would soon seem prophetic, that Gorbachev would respond, or that events in the Soviet Union would force him to respond. Within just a few years the wall that Kennedy had railed against as a tyrannical symbol, that Reagan had newly pointed to as an obvious sign of the failure of Communism, would indeed fall, along with the Soviet Union itself.

Population Density Today

The current population of the United States of America is estimated to be 308 million. More than 80 percent of its people live within urban areas—there are 51 cities with a population of more than 1 million. The west and south—especially California and Texas—are the main areas of population growth.

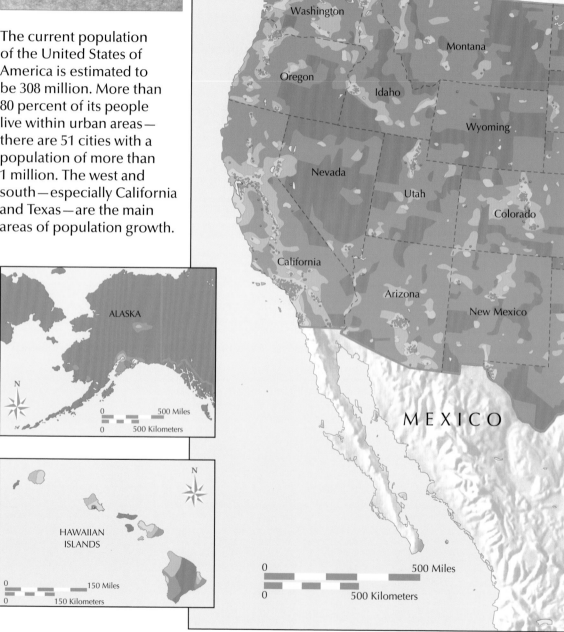

ALASKA

0 ——— 500 Miles
0 ——— 500 Kilometers

HAWAIIAN ISLANDS

0 ——— 150 Miles
0 ——— 150 Kilometers

0 ——— 500 Miles
0 ——— 500 Kilometers

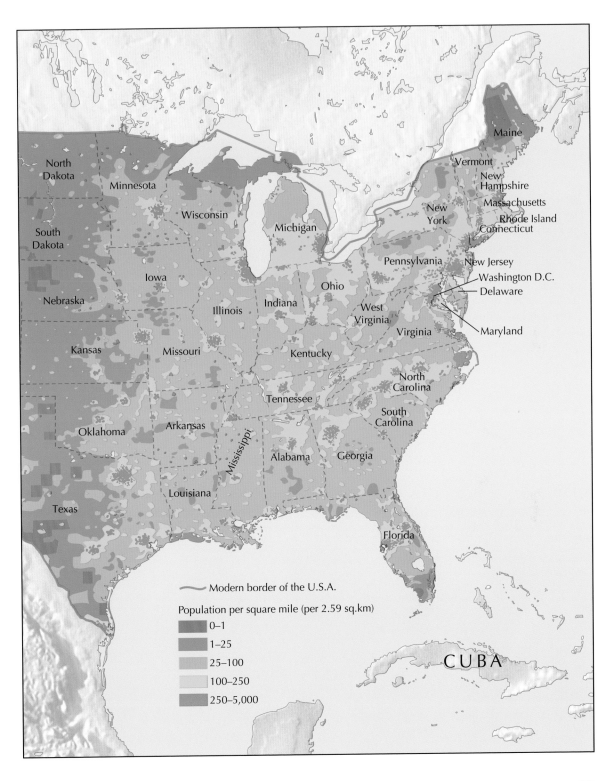

North Dakota

Minnesota

Wisconsin

Michigan

Maine

Vermont

New Hampshire

Massachusetts

Rhode Island

New York

Connecticut

South Dakota

Iowa

Pennsylvania

New Jersey

Washington D.C.

Delaware

Nebraska

Ohio

West Virginia

Illinois

Indiana

Maryland

Virginia

Kansas

Missouri

Kentucky

North Carolina

Tennessee

South Carolina

Oklahoma

Arkansas

Mississippi

Alabama

Georgia

Louisiana

Texas

Florida

Modern border of the U.S.A.

Population per square mile (per 2.59 sq.km)

0–1

1–25

25–100

100–250

250–5,000

C U B A

13

1
LBJ's America

The year 1963 had delivered great changes to the United States. In August the civil rights movement enjoyed its most inspirational moment as Dr. Martin Luther King Jr.—a Baptist minister from Montgomery, Alabama—delivered a landmark speech from the steps of the Lincoln Memorial in Washington, D.C., to a crowd numbering in the hundreds of thousands. Meanwhile, halfway across the world, America's fight to rescue South Vietnam from the threat of Communism was making little headway, as President Kennedy committed thousands of military advisers to train South Vietnamese troops. The leader of South Vietnam, Ngo Diem, had proven unpopular with his own people, so much so that Kennedy did not try to stop South Vietnamese army rebels from plotting to remove Diem from office. In the midst of that coup, the South Vietnamese president was assassinated.

A few weeks later, on November 22, Kennedy himself was killed by an assassin's bullet while visiting Dallas, leaving Americans stunned and in mourning. Just hours following the shooting of the president, Vice President Lyndon B. Johnson (LBJ), a former longtime congressman from West Texas, was sworn in onboard the presidential plane Air Force One with Kennedy's widow, Jackie, looking on. The Kennedy administration, with its youthful hopefulness, had represented a new opportunity to many of America's citizens. Now, with a new president at the helm, few people knew what direction the country would take.

JOHNSON AND VIETNAM

Almost from the beginning of his presidency Lyndon Johnson's foreign policy revolved around the increasingly uncontrollable conflict in Vietnam. The United States had been instrumental in the division of Vietnam during the early 1950s, when the country was a colony generally known as French Indochina. Communists took control of North Vietnam, and incursions into South Vietnam had begun when the North realized that the South would not agree to elections to determine the future of the whole of Vietnam. As 1963 turned into 1964, America's hand in Vietnam was a decade old. And the new president appeared committed to keeping his country's stake in Southeast Asia at all costs.

To a point, Johnson inherited that commitment, which had begun under President Eisenhower and expanded during the JFK years. In fact, America's support of South Vietnam had increased over the years so slowly, almost imperceptibly, that many Americans could not remember how exactly the U.S. obligations in the region had originally begun. However, Johnson was ready to take the U.S. involvement in Vietnam to any level necessary to contain Communism. When he became president in November 1963, the number of U.S. advisers in Vietnam was 16,000. These were non-combat personnel, there to train, not to participate directly in the fighting. During the first few months of LBJ's tenure in office, he decided to up the number of U.S. advisers by an additional 5,000 personnel and was already making plans for a further 5,000, as well.

At the end of the summer of 1964, with America's military commitment expanding at a decided rate, the playing field suddenly changed. In August the president announced on television that U.S. destroyers patrolling international waters in the Gulf of Tonkin, off the eastern shores of North Vietnam, had come under attack by North Vietnamese torpedo boats. Seemingly, several attacks had taken place at night but the details were sketchy— the North's boats were said to have run alongside the destroyers and strafed them with 50-caliber machine gunfire. Later investigations would raise questions about these incidents, including the extent of the damage and even where the "attacks" had taken place. It would appear afterward that the Johnson administration may not have accurately reported what had happened in the dark waters of the Gulf of Tonkin. Johnson, in addressing the U.S. people, had described the attacks as "unprovoked," but the destroyers in question had been supporting South Vietnamese raids against a pair of North Vietnamese islands, attacks which had been planned by U.S. military advisers.

Yet, President Johnson seized this opportunity to up the stakes in Vietnam. Claiming North Vietnamese aggression on the high seas, Johnson encouraged Congress to respond. Both Houses cooperated, passing a bill called the Gulf of Tonkin Resolution. The vote was extremely supportive, with a House tally of 416 to 0 and a Senate vote of 88 to 2. The resolution represented *carte blanche* for LBJ. It authorized the president to "take all necessary measures" to protect the lives of Americans in the region and to "prevent further aggression" in Southeast Asia. Armed with this piece of legislation, Johnson was now free, perhaps legally and morally, to escalate America's commitment in Vietnam without needing to ask Congress for a declaration of war. Over time many in Congress would come to regret the open-ended opportunity they had handed LBJ during those heated days in August.

CIVIL RIGHTS IN THE JOHNSON YEARS

Although John F. Kennedy had been slow to take up support of the expanding civil rights movement during the early 1960s, Lyndon B. Johnson proved an effective supporter indeed. Following Kennedy's death, LBJ pushed for the passage of another bill that had remained stuck in Congress, which was finally passed during his first full year in office—the Civil Rights Act of 1964.

Although earlier civil rights acts had been passed in U.S. history, some dating back to the 1860s and 70s, this act was the most far-reaching. It barred racial discrimination in such public places as hotels and restaurants, while calling for the Justice Department to file suits against schools that had not yet desegregated. This was even though the U.S. Supreme Court had ordered the schools to do so a decade earlier. Beyond the work of Johnson and the Congress, the civil rights movement was gaining further traction nationally. Dr. Martin Luther King Jr. was continuing to lead the march for equality, which gained him the Nobel Peace Prize in 1964. In 1965 the movement was in the midst of a campaign across the South to register 3 million new black voters. The drive soon focused on a march that spring from Selma, Alabama, to the state capital at Montgomery. With federal protection provided by President Johnson, the marchers could be counted in the tens of thousands, culminating in a total of 35,000 who stood outside the Alabama statehouse late in March to hear King deliver another of his stirring speeches.

The result of this hard-fought civil rights campaign was the Voting Rights Act of 1965, which Johnson supported. The act gave authority to the attorney general to provide federal officials to register voters, rather than relying exclusively on state officials.

AMERICA TAKES A COMBAT ROLE

President Johnson soon used the Gulf of Tonkin Resolution to commit U.S. ground troops to the Vietnam conflict. Following the election of 1964, which Johnson won in a land-

It also brought an end to literacy tests and other long-standing tricks created to deny blacks their right to vote.

Before the end of 1965 a quarter million blacks were registered to vote, the vast majority of them for the first time. For all these advances in the name of equality for blacks in America, the civil rights movement began to fragment in the mid-1960s. In August 1965, just days after the passage of the Voting Rights Act, the largely black district of Watts in Los Angeles exploded in race riots that killed 34 people and caused $35 million in property damage. The rampage erupted after a black motorist was arrested by a white highway patrolman, and it did not end until 14,000 National Guardsmen were called in.

Racial violence marked four "long hot summers" from 1965 to 1968, with rioting in many major U.S. cities. At the heart of these civil disturbances was a growing sense of outrage among blacks, who were tired of second-class citizenship and lack of opportunity. Paralleling this, a more militant element among the black community became highly critical of Dr. King's nonviolent approach to race issues. This movement's cry became "Black Power." It found a voice in such groups as the Black Muslims and the Black Panthers, who protested black athletes at the 1968 Olympic Games, and leaders such as Malcolm X and Stokely Carmichael, who called for segregation of blacks and whites. As historian George Tindall notes, one "Black Power" leader, H. Rap Brown, said: "We reject an American dream defined by white people and must work to construct an American reality defined by Afro-Americans."

Much of this radicalizing of black sentiment, which was always a fringe element, proved difficult for Dr. King and many of his followers to accept or understand.

slide vote against Arizona Senator Barry Goldwater, LBJ and his political advisers took those fateful steps.

On February 5, 1965, enemy guerrilla fighters, known as Viet Cong, attacked a U.S. military base at Pleiku, killing eight marines and wounding 126 additional U.S. forces. Before the week was over more attacks took place, indicating an upping of enemy action. Johnson seized this opportunity to escalate the war, ordering U.S. planes to carry out their first air assaults—referred to as "Rolling Thunder"—against North Vietnamese targets. The president said these

VIETNAM WAR ESCALATION 1963–1969

President Johnson was responsible for a major escalation of the war. As well as pouring increasing numbers of troops into the region, he subjected North Vietnam to a barrage of missiles, bombs, and rockets. During his term, more than 30,000 U.S. military personnel were killed.

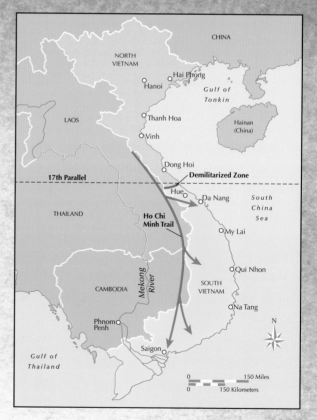

The map shows the major cities of Vietnam and the main routes of North Vietnamese troops moving south.

air strikes were necessary to stem the tide of enemy troop movements into South Vietnam, mostly along the so-called Ho Chi Minh Trail, which ran from North Vietnam through neighboring Laos and into South Vietnam. The bombing of North Vietnam would continue over the next seven years.

The following month the newly arrived U.S. Army commander, General William C. Westmoreland, called for ground troops to be used to protect U.S. air bases. What began as a trickle—two battalions of marines reached DaNang before the end of March—soon developed into an avalanche of U.S. fighting troops, with 100,000 of them in the country before the end of spring. By the end of summer, President Johnson had altered the nature of the U.S. commitment to South Vietnam. U.S. soldiers were now serving as combat troops.

"Limited War"

Troop numbers rose over the next few years to almost unimaginable levels. Before the end of 1965 more than 180,000 U.S. combat troops were in Vietnam. The following year that number had doubled. By the end of 1967 the U.S. military presence in Vietnam stood at over a half million troops. The jungles of South Vietnam were filled with U.S. patrols seeking enemy combatants. U.S. casualties increased with each passing year.

Meanwhile, the air assaults against the North continued on a massive scale. However, such targets as the North Vietnamese capital of Hanoi and the North's primary port, Haiphong, were kept off-limits, for fear of "escalating" the conflict to an uncontrollable level. Just as the U.S. police action in Korea had set the precedent of "limited war," so the U.S. strategy in Vietnam had its own limits. But bombs rained from the sky over other North Vietnamese targets, so much so that the total tonnage of bombs dropped in Vietnam surpassed that of all the theaters of war during World

War II. Vietnam was also the scene of such modern elements of war as tanks and chemical defoliants. Everywhere, it seemed, helicopters hovered above the action, the whirring of their blades a constant. Casualties mounted. By the spring of 1966, 4,000 Americans had been killed in the country.

During the battle of Dak To in South Vietnam in November 1967 members of the U.S. Airborne Brigade load casualties onto a Red Cross helicopter for evacuation to a field hospital.

AN UNCONVENTIONAL CONFLICT

Between 1965 and 1972, U.S. combat forces remained in Vietnam, becoming increasingly drawn into in a war that seemed destined never to be won. It was difficult for many Americans to understand the true nature of the war. The United States delivered to Vietnam all its latest military innovations and technologies. Many of these, though, were designed for conventional battles and for use against conventional enemy troops. However the North Vietnamese, and especially the Viet Cong (South Vietnamese supporters of Communism), were not fighting a conventional war. Civilian populations in the South were infiltrated with enemy forces and supporters. Most enemy fighters did not wear standard uniforms; they used hit-and-run, guerrilla tactics, and could easily blend in with civilians. They were armed with AK-47 assault rifles and were highly mobile, carrying little equipment, save for a sack with limited food and ammunition. The enemy dug tunnels and sanctuaries underground, making them even more difficult for U.S. patrols to uncover.

In the actual fighting, U.S. forces won most of the major battles and the after-battle reports indicated that, despite a constant U.S. casualty list, for every American death there were many more Communist forces killed. However, the number of enemy deaths did not seem to make a difference in the Communists' overall commitment to the war. Ho Chi Minh himself had stated as much during the 1940s, when he and his followers were fighting their French colonialists, notes historian George Tindall: "You can kill ten of my men for every one I kill of yours, but even at those odds, you will lose and I will win."

Thus, even as the United States, with support from its South Vietnamese comrades, was "winning" in the field, the war was not turning in their favor. The war was neither being won nor lost—simply extended, year after year. With the passing of those years, field commanders and Pentagon offi-cials urged President Johnson to commit to more resources, more manpower, and heavier air bombing. Some encour-aged the expansion of the war into neighboring countries in Southeast Asia, such as Laos and Cambodia, where enemy forces often conveniently hid to escape. A handful of frus-trated commanders even suggested using nuclear weapons, just as had been proposed during the Korean conflict. Ulti-mately, Johnson did not pursue any of these latter options, even as the war continued to worsen and his popularity at home fell. By 1967 America seemed at war with itself.

THE CONFLICT AT HOME

By that fall opposition to the war was on the rise. Some groups organized peace marches and demonstrations against the war in major cities such as Washington and New York, and the public became aware of a significant antiwar move-ment. Most Americans kept up with the war by watching the evening news on television. Now, increasingly, journal-ists gave their own support to the antiwar movement by fil-ing negative reports about the brutal nature of the conflict and the seeming futility of America's role. Major magazines, including *Time* and *Newsweek*, printed editorials urging the end of the war. Then the popular anchorman of the *CBS Evening News*, Walter Cronkite, announced that he no lon-ger believed the Vietnam War could be won by the United States. His proclamation signaled to Johnson that he had lost middle America. In response, LBJ had to admit: "If I've lost Walter, then it's over. I've lost Mr. Average Citizen."

Support was crumbling around Johnson. In March 1968 Robert McNamara, Johnson's secretary of defense, resigned his office. McNamara, who had helped establish a signifi-cant U.S. presence in Vietnam during the Kennedy admin-istration, had decided the war was a mistake, a conflict that

America could not win. In his words: "The picture of the world's greatest superpower killing or injuring 1,000 non-combatants a week, while trying to pound a tiny backward nation into submission on an issue whose merits are hotly disputed, is not a pretty one." Meanwhile George Kennan, who had advised President Truman during the 1940s and had coined the term "containment" for limiting the advance of Communism, testified in 1966 before the Senate Foreign Relations Committee that this policy really applied to Europe, not to Southeast Asia. With the president's popularity rating having plummeted to 35 percent by the spring of 1968, the Vietnam War had become Johnson's albatross.

JOHNSON'S DOMESTIC AGENDA

During his first administration the president was never able to turn his full attention away from the conflict in Vietnam, yet he did manage to pursue a significant agenda at home. In the wake of Kennedy's death, LBJ took advantage of the situation to push a political agenda that Kennedy had largely failed to get through Congress. Suddenly, bills that had been tied up in Congress made their way to the floor and a flood of legislation soon followed.

Heading Johnson's agenda were tax reductions and civil rights bills, plus a cause that soon became uniquely linked to LBJ—his so-called "War on Poverty." Recent studies by, among others, socialist Michael Harrington, had indicated that as many as 40 to 50 million Americans were stuck in a cycle of poverty, living lives with no hope of change or improvement. Johnson himself knew something about being poor. He had grown up in a small Texas town, Johnson City, with no indoor plumbing or electricity.

Paid for with the economic growth brought about by $10 billion in tax cuts, Johnson's domestic war on poverty took several fronts. Congress passed his Economic Opportunity

Bill, which established a Job Corps for inner-city young people and a program called Head Start, designed to give a leg-up to underprivileged preschoolers. There was funding for a work–study program for college students in need, farm grants, and support for small, rural businesses. Those hiring the "chronic unemployed" received government loans. Johnson implemented Volunteers in Service to America (VISTA), which constituted a sort of Peace Corps at home. Also there was the Community Action Program, which empowered poor communities to design and implement programs to better serve their own needs.

All this social retooling and enfranchising of the poor was labeled, by Johnson, his "Great Society Program." In a speech in Ann Arbor, Michigan, the president stated that his programs were built on "abundance and liberty for all. The Great Society demands an end to poverty and racial injustice, to which we are fully committed in our time."

JOHNSON'S 1964 MANDATE

Less than a year after Kennedy's death LBJ faced his own presidential election. The passage of several acts in support of his domestic agenda, along with his commitment to continue supporting the South Vietnamese struggle against Communism, enabled Johnson to campaign on a legacy of clear, political successes.

The 1964 election proved lively, as the conservative Republican candidate, Senator Barry Goldwater, a wealthy department store magnate, pounded Johnson for his actions in Vietnam. He accused the president of pursuing a limited, "no-win" approach to the war, even as he strongly indicated that he would apply limitless bombing against North Vietnam to force the enemy into submission. Goldwater also lambasted LBJ's domestic agenda, which he likened to Roosevelt's New Deal, referring to Johnson as the "Santa Claus of the free lunch." The Arizona senator promised to sell off the government's Tennessee Valley Authority (TVA) projects to private investors. He raised doubts about whether Social Security should be continued. The outspoken conservative Goldwater felt free to speak his mind at every turn and the Republicans created a slogan to reassure the public: "In your heart, you know he's right."

But Goldwater's positions raised questions for many middle-of-the-road Americans. His call to step up the bombing in Vietnam made him look like a warmonger. Johnson took advantage of his Republican challenger's militaristic talk by making a public promise: "We are not about to send American boys nine or ten thousand miles from home to do what Asian boys ought to be doing for themselves." Goldwater's conservatism had led him to vote against a ban on nuclear testing, and against civil rights legislation. For so many voters, the man from Arizona appeared to lean too far to the right. The Democrats came up with an official slogan to counterbalance that of the Republicans: "In your guts, you know he's nuts." As a result, President Johnson took the 1964 election with 61 percent of the vote.

NEW SOCIAL LEGISLATION

Feeling armed with a mandate from the American voter, Johnson was in a hurry to press for new legislation to further his "Great Society" agenda. Not since Franklin Roosevelt's first "Hundred Days" had Congress seen such a flurry of action. High on Johnson's list of priorities were changes in government healthcare that had been proposed during the Truman years to no avail. The president was able to steamroll legislation through, with many Republicans getting onboard, to create the Medicare system, which provided medical care for Americans over the age of 65. Another part of the legislation called for Medicaid—a plan to provide states with federal grant monies to help pay for care for citizens who were unable to afford for it themselves. Within days of submitting the bills for these programs to Congress, Johnson proposed further legislation to provide $1.5 billion in education aid for elementary and secondary schools.

Once these bills passed, a whirlwind of additional bills followed. In total, Johnson's Great Society proposals took the form of 435 separate bills, including the 1966 Appalachian Regional Development Act ($1.1 billion) to boost the standard of living among the region's poor; the Housing and Urban Development Act of 1965, to build nearly a quarter million new homes (the bill also created a cabinet level department of the same name, whose first secretary became the first black cabinet member); and urban renewal plans with a price tag of nearly $3 billion. Congress also passed the Highway Safety Act and the Traffic Safety Act to establish safety standards for car manufacturers and highway planners. For college students, Johnson saw passage of the Higher Education Act, which provided financial support to college students.

In 1965 Congress passed the Immigration Act, which had been shaped during the Kennedy administration but failed to pass until Johnson revived it. The act, which did not take effect until 1968, created an immigration policy limiting immigrants from outside the Western Hemisphere to 170,000 annually and from within the Americas to 120,000 annually. Given an increasing trend among Western Europeans to immigrate in fewer numbers to the United States, the country soon witnessed a significant increase in the numbers of Asians and Latin Americans, especially from such nations as Mexico, the Dominican Republic, the Philippines, and Korea. Yet even as such legislation trumpeted the successes of the Johnson administration, the war in Vietnam continued to drag on.

2
The Nixon Years

The year 1968 would prove to be one the most difficult, challenging, and divisive in twentieth-century U.S. history. The war in Vietnam was already a focal point of dissent among an increasing number of Americans, as the conflict dragged on with thousands of U.S. military personnel dying in a military action that seemed unsinkable. In the Vietnamese village of My Lai, a U.S. infantry unit led by Lieutenant William Calley executed at least 200 people, including women and children, and dumped their bodies in a mass grave. At home, race riots continued to rage in U.S. cities from the East to the West Coast. It was a year of assassination as a stunned nation struggled to cope with the deaths of Dr. Martin Luther King in Memphis in April and of Robert Kennedy, JFK's younger brother, in Los Angeles, just two months later. Off the coast of Korea, the North Koreans captured a U.S. Navy intelligence-gathering ship, the *Pueblo*, and held the crew captive. That summer political rioting unfolded in the streets of Chicago during the Democratic National Convention. The year 1968 was also an election year—one that would, amidst all the violence, usher out the Johnson administration and bring former Vice President Richard Nixon to the White House.

SPINNING OUT OF CONTROL

At the beginning of 1968 the war in Vietnam was a disaster. Despite more than three years of fighting involving U.S. ground troops, the enemy was nowhere near being defeated. On January 31—the first day of the Vietnamese New Year, called Tet—Communist forces opened a large-scale offensive throughout South Vietnam. The Tet Offensive was so successful that enemy forces made their way to the streets of Saigon, the South Vietnamese capital.

Although U.S. and South Vietnamese forces eventually turned the Tet Offensive around, its short-lived success convinced a greater number of Americans that the war was lost. As a result the antiwar element in the States grew dramatically. Many Americans were disenchanted with a war that was costing, by 1968, $300,000 for every enemy killed, while, despite Johnson's Great Society, at home the federal government was only spending $88 per person on poverty programs. Within weeks of Tet, public opposition to the war had doubled.

Johnson's presidency was just another casualty of the Vietnam War. With an approval rating of just 35 percent, he finally announced on March 31 that he would not seek reelection. In the wake of Johnson's announcement, his vice president, Minnesotan Hubert Humphrey decided to enter the race. But Humphrey already faced stiff opposition from other strong Democratic front-runners, especially Robert Kennedy, brother of the late JFK, who had declared his candidacy just days earlier.

Two Assassinations

Then, on April 4, Dr. Martin Luther King was shot and killed on the second-story balcony of a Memphis motel. The minister who had led the civil rights movement was dead. Outraged and disappointed blacks across the country rioted in 100 cities, resulting in 43 deaths, 3,000 injuries, and 27,000 arrests.

With little time for recovery, the nation was further shocked on June 6 when Robert Kennedy was assassinated in a Los Angeles hotel ballroom after he had just won the California Democratic primary. In less than five years two Kennedy brothers had been gunned down. A speechwriter for Robert Kennedy, Jack Newfield, wrote words that rang

Coretta Scott King attends the funeral ceremonies for her husband. Musician, author, and civil rights activist Harry Belafonte sits beside Mrs. King, who wears a veil. Daughter Bernice Albertine King stands in front.

true for many who had hung their hopes on such charismatic and committed political figures, notes historian Klaus P. Fischer:

> *Things were not really getting better . . . we shall not overcome . . . We had already glimpsed the most compassionate leaders our nation could produce [King and the two Kennedys], and they had all been assassinated. And from this time forward, things would get worse: Our best political leaders were part of memory now, not hope.*

To some, the very fabric of American society seemed to be unraveling.

NIXON: THE LAW AND ORDER CANDIDATE

The summer of 1968 saw additional rioting as the two major political parties prepared to gather for their conventions. In Chicago the Democrats selected Hubert Humphrey. For many in the antiwar movement, Humphrey only represented a continuation of Johnson's policies in Vietnam. Outside the convention hall, protesters staged several demonstrations, provoking Chicago Mayor Richard Daley to order 24,000 police (National Guardsmen were later called in) to the streets to arrest the protesters. Television cameras filmed the confrontations, which included bloody riots, the police wielding billy clubs and lobbing tear gas canisters, as demonstrators taunted them with a repeated jeer: "The whole world is watching." It was all ironic to so many: the proceedings of the generally liberal Democratic Party facing protests from a generation of disenchanted young Americans.

Following the ugly violence and confrontational political strife in Chicago, which signaled great splits among supporters of the Democratic Party, the Republicans met at their convention in Miami and nominated Richard Nixon. The former vice president, who had cut his political teeth during the late 1940s and early 1950s, was making a political comeback.

Having served as Eisenhower's vice president, Nixon had lost the 1960 election to Kennedy and was then defeated for the governorship of California in 1962. Following that loss he had announced his retirement from politics. He jabbed reporters, whom he believed had presented him unfairly to the public, with the line: "You won't have Nixon to kick around any more." But this promise to put political ambitions aside was short-lived, as he campaigned for Goldwater in 1964 and remained in the mainstream of Republican politics to follow. Now it was 1968 and Nixon was ready to run. As he opened his campaign he spoke to the press, telling them he was "tanned, ready, and rested," a reference to his poor and pale showing during the televised debates with Kennedy back in 1960.

Nixon saw his opportunity that year in the face of Johnson's declining popularity. With Humphrey soon cast as a Johnson "insider," Nixon campaigned on contrasts. He spoke directly to the American middle class—whom he referred to as the "Silent Majority"—many of whom had prospered and put down family roots during the 1950s when he and Ike had been in the White House. He promised stability in a turbulent age; "law and order" in the face of riots and sometimes violent political protests; and "peace with honor" in Vietnam. Nixon tapped a vein of conservative concern across the country.

A Third Party Candidate

But some conservatives were not satisfied with the Nixon candidacy and turned instead to a third campaigner, Governor George C. Wallace of Alabama. Wallace had gained a national reputation during the early 1960s for strongly opposing integration at the University of Alabama. On one occasion he actually stood in the door of a university building to block the way of black students trying to enter. Wallace now proved to be a rough-edged, no-nonsense populist, running on the American Independent Party ticket. He spoke with disdain, claiming "liberals, intellectuals, and long-hairs have run the country for too long," and vowed, if elected, to "throw all these phonies and their briefcases into the Potomac." The Alabama Governor said he would halt forced busing to achieve school integration, jail welfare "cheaters," and crack down on race rioters and antiwar demonstrators.

Wallace's promise of "law and order" lay far to the right of Nixon's. He also announced his intent to upscale the war in Vietnam. His candidacy took on even more ominous tones when he added retired air force general Curtis LeMay as his vice presidential running mate. In October, LeMay frightened some Americans when he told reporters that the U.S. military should "bomb the North Vietnamese back into the Stone Age," then added, without Wallace's approval: "I think there are many times when it would be most efficient to use nuclear weapons."

The Election Results

Ultimately, Wallace's candidacy probably did not impact the outcome of the 1968 election, which Nixon won by a narrow margin of the popular vote over Humphrey—43.4 percent to 42.7 percent, a gap of just 500,000 votes. Wallace had gained an impressive 13.5 percent of the popular vote, carrying five southern states and 46 electoral ballots. Yet even though Wallace was actually a Southern Democrat, he likely did not pull away that many votes from Humphrey, as those supporting the Alabama Governor tended to be rather conservative. If anything, Nixon likely lost votes to Wallace's third party candidacy. It should be noted, though, that Nixon's and Wallace's combined votes totaled 57 percent, so the U.S. electorate had spoken clearly: The vast majority of voters were interested in stability, rather than the change that Johnson had delivered in his Great Society programs.

NIXON AND THE VIETNAM WAR

Nixon entered the White House in January 1969, ready to reestablish that sought-after stability, both at home and in his foreign policy. This included his strategies concerning the Vietnam War. He was concerned that the outcome of the war had been hampered by strategy and an over-reliance on the contributions of the U.S. military. In his State of the Union address in 1970, Nixon spoke of helping Americans to pursue "the lift of a driving dream." In defining his words later, he said that, before that could happen, "We have to get rid of the nightmares we inherited. One of those nightmares

GRUESOME STATISTICS

Just as the Vietnam War became unpopular at home, so the soldiers assigned to duty in Vietnam also became less supportive of the conflict. For many people, the number of deaths was sobering. In 1965, the first year that U.S. combat troops served in Vietnam, 636 Americans were killed. The following year the total number killed was more than ten times as many—6,644. In 1967 the U.S. death toll passed the 16,000 mark. By 1968, when protest against the war was steadily rising, the number of U.S. forces killed in Vietnam had reached 30,610.

Steadily, the commitment of U.S. troops in Vietnam began to waver. In 1966 the desertion rate among U.S. soldiers was 15 per 1,000. Five years later the desertion rate had increased almost five times over, to 74 per 1,000. Incidents of soldiers being AWOL (Absent Without Leave) also increased, from 57 per 1,000 in 1966 to 176 per 1,000 by 1971.

is a war without end." Unfortunately, even as Nixon altered the U.S. commitment to the war, he found himself limited in his options for ending the conflict by his campaign promise of "peace with honor." As an old Cold Warrior, Nixon had long doted on issues relating to foreign policy, which tended to interest him much more than domestic policies and politics. To formulate not only a new course for the war, but a new course for U.S. diplomacy, Nixon came to rely heavily on Harvard professor Henry Kissinger. Kissinger was German-born, but his family had immigrated to the United States when he was a teenager. Raised in New York City, Kissinger had attended George Washington High School at night while he worked in a shaving brush factory during the day. Known as an expert in history and diplomacy, Kissinger was appointed by Nixon as special assistant for national security affairs.

The policy hammered out between Nixon and Kissinger concerning Vietnam took several avenues. Both men were intent on reducing the increasing level of U.S. distaste for the war. One significant area of dissatisfaction centered on the drafting of young men for military service. Nixon changed the selection system to a "lottery," in which officials would draw the birthdates of all 19-year-old males and assign them numbers between 1 and 365. Those whose numbers were low would be subject to the draft. Eventually, Nixon pushed for an all-volunteer army, which finally became reality in 1973. By then, the war was over.

A Reduction in Troops

The most important change that Nixon brought to the war in 1969 was a policy he called "Vietnamization." Since 1965 the South Vietnamese had relied on increasing numbers of U.S. soldiers to fight their war for them. Nixon's new policy emphasized training and equipping the South Vietnamese military, while pulling significant numbers of Americans out of the country, with the goal of ultimately turning the war over to the Vietnamese military.

At the end of his first six months in office, Nixon announced the withdrawal of 60,000 U.S. ground forces from Vietnam, representing the first drop in U.S. troop strength since the start of the war. Through the remainder of his first term, Nixon pulled troops out of Vietnam. By the fall of 1972 the number of U.S. military personnel in Vietnam had plummeted from a Johnson-era high of 540,000 to just 60,000. The drawdown did quiet, to a point, street-level opposition to the war, but it did not succeed as a policy. Despite peace talks through those same years in Paris, which were halted in 1969 due to arguments over the shape of the table where negotiators would sit, the North Vietnamese constantly dragged their heels.

Cambodia

Yet even as Nixon pulled U.S. forces out of the war, he and Kissinger pursued an escalation policy by taking the conflict into neighboring Cambodia. Their intent was reasonable. For years the North Vietnamese and the South Vietnamese Viet Cong had used Cambodia as a shelter, launching attacks against U.S. forces, then scurrying across the border to Cambodian territory. Nixon now ordered "Operation Menu," which included air strikes to destroy enemy bases on Cambodian soil. As would become his *modus operandi*, the president did not seek authorization from Congress for this action and kept his alteration in policy a secret.

Over a period of 14 months, U.S. planes dropped a total of 100,000 tons (91,000 metric tons) of bombs over Cambodia—four times the bomb tonnage dropped on Japan during World War II. In late April 1970, after a regime change in Cambodia which brought pro-U.S. military leaders to power, Nixon went on television and spoke to the American people, informing them he was ordering U.S. troops into Cambodia to "clean out" enemy bases that were being used for "increased military aggression."

ANTIWAR PROTESTS

Part of most antiwar demonstrations were "peace marches" that invariably ended with confrontations between police and demonstrators. Some of the demonstrations led to riots, as at the Democratic National Convention in August 1968, held to nominate a successor to Lyndon B. Johnson.

Student antiwar demonstrators offer flowers to National Guardsmen as symbols of peace.

PROTESTS AT HOME

If the antiwar movement had become less vocal in 1969, it exploded again in 1970. Demonstrations spread across the country, often centered on college and university campuses, including Ohio's Kent State University. There a student demonstration, which included the burning of the campus ROTC building, ended tragically after National Guardsmen opened fire on antiwar demonstrators, killing four college students. Although most Americans polled thought the students in question "had only got what they asked for" by their actions on the Kent State campus, the tenor of support for the war was dwindling fast.

In December Congress repealed the Gulf of Tonkin Resolution, which had originally authorized U.S. ground troops in Vietnam. Meanwhile nearly two of every three Americans asked in public opinion polls favored the complete withdrawal of U.S. troops from the war. Perhaps a peripheral result of the youth protests against the war was the ratification of the Twenty-Sixth Amendment in 1971, which lowered the minimum voting age from 21 to 18. Those protesting the war had complained that they could be drafted at 18, even though they did not have the right to vote.

However, completely abandoning the war was never in Nixon's game plan. In early 1971 he put Vietnamization to the true test by ordering U.S. air forces to only assist a force of exclusively South Vietnamese ground troops in an invasion of neighboring Laos. Weeks later those same troops scrambled back to their home country in defeat. The North Vietnamese followed this failure a year later with their largest offensive of the war, the so-called Easter Offensive. While combined U.S. and South Vietnamese forces were able to turn this new offensive around, as they had the Tet Offensive four years earlier, the situation was interpreted by some Americans as the case that Vietnamization had not worked.

With 1972 an election year, Nixon faced the continuing specter of Vietnam as Johnson had four years earlier. Determined to turn the war in his favor, the president authorized, for the first time, the U.S. bombing of Hanoi, the North Vietnamese capital, and the North's principal port, Haiphong, plus the mining of seven North Vietnamese ports, including Haiphong. These steps were designed to place new pressures on the North—something that the Vietnamization of ground troops had failed to achieve during Nixon's entire first term.

PEACE TALKS START

Meanwhile, Henry Kissinger was meeting privately in Paris with his North Vietnamese counterpart, Foreign Secretary Le Duc Tho, to hammer out a ceasefire agreement. On October 26, with the election looming, Kissinger made a public announcement: that he and Tho were near an agreement and that "peace is at hand." At the heart of the agreement was Kissinger's dropping of a longstanding demand that all North Vietnamese troops must leave South Vietnam before an agreement could be made. Hope sprang for many voters and Nixon was elected over Democratic challenger George McGovern by a landslide, the popular vote coming in at 60.7 to 37.5 percent. McGovern, who had campaigned in complete opposition to the war, only received 17 electoral votes to Nixon's 520! The South Dakota senator had proven far too liberal for many U.S. voters.

End of a Controversial War

With reelection behind him, Nixon continued to press the North for an agreement. But the problem proved to be the leader of South Vietnam, Nguyen Van Thieu, who was not happy with Kissinger's surrender of the removal of North Vietnamese troops from the South at the point of a ceasefire. Then, in mid-December, talks with the North Vietnamese broke down, leading Nixon to order renewed levels of U.S. bombing over the North. For nearly two weeks, beginning on December 17, the United States carried out the "Christmas Bombings," with U.S. B-52s dropping their highest levels of ordinance since the start of the war. However, 15 of these bombers were shot down by the North Vietnamese in this period, compared to only one previous downing during the entire war. On December 30 Nixon ordered a halt to the bombing, and North Vietnam took the opportunity to return to the peace talks table.

On January 27, 1973, all sides signed an "agreement on ending the war and restoring peace in Vietnam." (President Thieu only agreed to this after significant pressure.) A cease-fire was immediately put into effect. Just two months later, on March 29, the last remaining U.S. combat troops were flown out of South Vietnam. After eight years of ground fighting and nearly 20 years of U.S. support for the South, America's war in Vietnam had ended.

This war had become one of the most controversial in U.S. history. As with earlier U.S. wars, including the Mexican War, domestic opposition had reached a level of crescendo. When the smoke of the war had cleared, the conflict had cost blood and treasure that included 58,000 deaths, 300,000 injured personnel, and $150 billion. Whether the United States had salvaged South Vietnam from Communism was not even clear as the war ended, but over the following two years North Vietnamese forces continued to battle for the South until they succeeded in bringing down its government. In late April 1975 (when Nixon was out of office, and Gerald Ford was president) Communist forces overran Saigon. U.S. diplomatic personnel evacuated the country's embassy in the South's capital by helicopter, representing the end of a longstanding U.S. presence in Vietnam.

3

The Fall of Richard Nixon

On July 20, 1969, *Apollo 11* landed on the Moon, and Neil Armstrong became the first person to set foot on its surface, achieving the goal that President Kennedy had set for the nation's space program earlier in the decade. The United States had pursued its space program during the 1950s and 1960s as an extension of the Cold War, competing with the Soviet Union to achieve success in space. Following the lunar landing, the space race had little relevance as a part of U.S. foreign policy.

President Nixon intended to establish something of a new international order through his foreign policy efforts. Although Nixon had cut his political teeth during the early days of the Cold War and had been staunchly anti-Communist, he had now come to believe that new strategies were necessary in dealing with the Soviets. Earlier presidential policies, such as Truman's "Containment," had hinged on a "bipolar" world in which the two superpowers dominated.

Nixon tried to alter U.S. foreign policy toward a "multipolar" model, one that recognized such previously secondary forces as Western Europe, Japan, and China.

NIXON AND DÉTENTE

By the late 1960s China had been a Communist state for 20 years. Nixon was prepared to open a dialogue with the most populous of the Asian powers, but part of his strategy was to play the Chinese Communists off the Soviet Communists. In July 1971 he sent Henry Kissinger on a secret mission to Beijing. The result was an invitation to Nixon to visit China—the first such opportunity ever for a standing U.S. president. In February 1972 Nixon paid his formal call. He met with Chinese officials, posed for pictures at the Great Wall, and negotiated behind closed doors. One of the results of the negotiations was the U.S. agreement to expel representatives of Nationalist China (Taiwan) from the United Nations and replace them with those of the People's Republic.

Prior to sidling up to the Chinese, Nixon was already at work establishing closer relations with the Soviets, a policy referred to as *détente*. During Nixon's first year in office, diplomats from the United States and Soviet Union met in Helsinki, Finland, to discuss limiting nuclear weapons. In 1972 those talks produced the first Strategic Arms Limitation Treaty, known as SALT I, which froze some categories of nuclear weapons, such as intercontinental ballistic missiles (ICBMs), at their then-existing levels.

THE NIXON DOCTRINE

While working closely with such superpowers as the Soviet Union and Communist China was important to Nixon's foreign policy, he also worked to build better relations with various developing countries, but without committing to them excessively, as the United States had done in Vietnam. The result was the creation of the "Nixon Doctrine," by which the United States agreed to "participate in the defense and development of allies and friends" in the Developing World, while leaving the "basic responsibility" for their future to those nations themselves. There was to be no new Vietnam to hang around the neck of the United States.

One region in which the Nixon Doctrine played itself out was the Middle East, where Israel represented America's most important ally. In October 1973, on the Jewish high holy day of Yom Kippur, Egyptian and Syrian forces attacked Israel. The Israelis had already fought their Arab neighbors six years earlier. Then, an Egyptian invasion ended just six days later with an Israeli victory—a conflict that became known as the "Six Day War." This new invasion teetered back and forth for 10 days, as the Israelis first struggled after the surprise incursion, then gained ground and launched a counter-offensive that sent the Egyptians dashing back across the Sinai Peninsula with Israeli tanks in pursuit. Yet the United States, intent on defusing the conflict, pressured the Israeli government to accept a ceasefire rather than push the Egyptians any further. Partially at stake for America was continuing access to Arab oil. The war ended and the United States had gained three insights: That it could not support only Israel and disregard the Arab world; that oil could be used as a weapon against the western industrialized nations; and that the days of cheap, easy access to this vital natural resource might be at an end.

AN ECONOMY IN TURMOIL

Oil not only played a role in America's changing foreign policy—the price of this crucial commodity was also having an impact on the U.S. economy. By the early 1970s the U.S. economic system was already in the throes of a serious downturn. The golden economy of the 1950s and early

1960s had played out, thrown off the rails by the sheer cost of Johnson's Great Society, the black hole of the Vietnam War, and rising oil prices. Inflation was the economic factor that impacted the largest number of Americans during Nixon's first term. The federal deficit kept increasing, while a lack of inexpensive commodities, such as metals and oil, was hampering America's capacity to carry on business as usual. For the first time in the twentieth century, Developing World nations who were rich in natural resources were beginning to figure out the true value of these raw materials.

Leading the way was the international cartel called the Organization of Petroleum Exporting Countries (OPEC). Its members were the world's largest oil-producing states and included several countries in the Middle East and Africa. During the Yom Kippur War Arab members of OPEC decided they would cut off oil exports to states who supported Israel, including the United States. Simultaneously OPEC raised the price of oil by 500 percent, from $3 per barrel to $15, which spread economic chaos throughout the western nations. The international playing field was in the midst of a serious shift of power.

Inflation and Unemployment

Nixon was not interested in domestic issues. They tended to bore him, and he was certainly no economist. Having made conservative appointments to the Federal Reserve Board, Nixon had guaranteed higher interest rates, accompanied by a shrinking money supply, neither of which made a dent in inflation. Between 1969 and the summer of 1971 the cost of living rose by 15 percent. Unemployment also rose during Nixon's first two years in office, from 3.5 percent to just shy of 6 percent. It was all contradictory—a combination of higher prices and a stagnant economy—and led to the coining of a new economic term, "stagflation."

"Turn on, Tune in, Drop Out"

During the late 1960s a new counterculture took shape. Its participants were labeled "hippies," and they became identified with protest and defiance of authority. Despite their drive to express themselves uniquely, the costume of the hippies was almost universal, consisting of long hair, beards, blue jeans (which many older Americans associated with radicals of the 1930s and 1940s), tie-dyed shirts in dizzying patterns, sandals, and a general scruffiness. Hippies were also among those directly connected with the country's developing drug culture.

Many hippies were the products of middle-class or affluent U.S. families. They were disenchanted with the Vietnam War, a government they did not trust, racism, and a perceived greedy corporate America. They refused to be a part of the system. Harvard Professor Timothy Leary, who had been involved in some of the early experimentation with the mind-altering hallucinogenic drug LSD, had some singular advice for the nation's youth: "Turn on to the scene, tune in to what's happening, and drop out."

The hippies were more than happy to oblige. Seeking to redefine themselves from mainstream America, some hippies studied Oriental mystic religions, such as Buddhism. Others made a near career of dabbling with hallucinogenics. Communes sprang up across the country, while the Haight-Ashbury district in San Francisco and New York's East Village became the new meccas for hippies. While hippies experimented with a variety of illegal drugs, the common drug of choice for many was marijuana.

Much of the popular music of the late 1960s involved lyrics that mirrored the world of the hippies. Rock music concerts gave young people an opportunity to come together and groove to lyrics that suggested protest, drug use, and free love. The most iconic concert was held for three days in August 1969. The Woodstock Music Festival unfolded on a 600-acre (240-hectare) farm outside Bethel, New York. Organizers had expected only a few thousands of attendees, but a half million curious young people showed up. Rain turned the grounds into mud, as popular musicians such as Joe Cocker; Jimi Hendrix; the Grateful Dead; Creedence Clearwater Revival; Jefferson Airplane; and Crosby, Stills, Nash, and Young rocked the rural setting. Woodstock became a kinetic scene of open drug use and free expression.

Generally, the hippie movement should be viewed separately from the more radical youth-oriented groups that were springing up in America by the early 1960s. Perhaps the earliest group was Students for a Democratic Society (SDS), formed in 1960 at the University of Michigan by Tom Hayden and Al Haber. The SDS began protesting a lack of individual freedom and opportunity for singular expression. When he and his followers were referred to as Communists, Hayden coined the term "New Left," to distinguish his group, which sought the goal of participatory, grassroots democracy, from old-line Marxists.

Those representing the hardcore "New Left" included a group established in 1964 at the University of California-Berkeley called the Free Speech Movement (FSM). By the late 1960s the SDS and FSM were organizing students across the country, as well as others, to protest the Vietnam War. A march in the spring of 1967 featured a half million protesters gathered in New York's Central Park, where young men flicked Bic lighters and burned their draft cards. ("Draft cards" were issued by the federal government's Selective Service to young men who were required to register for possible military service when they turned 18.)

In 1968 the SDS split apart into rival groups, including an extreme underground organization called the Weathermen. They took their name from a song by folk musician Bob Dylan: "You don't need a weatherman to know which way the wind blows." Between 1969 and 1970 the Weathermen engaged in a spree of political protests that included fire-bombing university and federal government buildings. By 1971 the New Left had lost much of its wind and petered out as a political movement. Several of those who had protested the Vietnam War and sought radical change in America became part of the budding environmental movement that remains active today.

In 1971 Nixon issued an executive order establishing a 90-day freeze on wages and prices, then set mandatory guidelines for both in November. Such moves did not fix the recession. And once wage and price controls were finally lifted, prices simply went up again. In 1973 prices increased by 9 percent. Then in 1974, following the oil embargo and a rise in oil prices, they increased by 12 percent. Facing serious oil shortages, the Nixon administration struggled with a suitable policy and found few answers. A desperate government lowered highway speeds to 55 miles per hour (88 kilometers per hour) and pushed for office thermostats to be set at 68°F (20°C). Long lines at gas stations became the norm in many U.S. cities. Not only did the recession plague Nixon's presidency, but the economic malaise continued through the terms of the next two presidents to follow.

WATERGATE

In the early morning hours of June 17, 1972, Washington Metro Police arrested five men who were attempting to burglarize the offices of the Democratic National Committee in the Watergate Complex in Washington, D.C. The burglars were caught with sophisticated electronic bugging devices, pen-sized tear-gas guns, and $2,300 in cash, the majority in consecutively numbered $100 bills. When the media reported the story, it drew only curious attention from the public.

Then two young reporters for *The Washington Post*, Carl Bernstein and Bob Woodward, investigated the backgrounds of the accused burglars and made an interesting discovery. The leader of the group, James W. McCord, Jr., had once worked for the Central Intelligence Agency (CIA) and had more recently been employed by the Committee to Reelect the President (often called CREEP). The reporters also determined that the burglars had been paid out of a secret CREEP fund, controlled by members of Nixon's White House staff.

Immediately Nixon and his staff denied any connection to the burglars. The case came to trial in early 1973 and, through prodding by federal Judge John J. Sirica, McCord agreed to tell what he knew. By that time a special Senate investigating committee had been established under Senator Sam J. Ervin of North Carolina to determine whether there was a connection between the alleged burglars and the White House. Once McCord began to testify, others joined him, which led to a flood of confessions.

Soon events and the words of several people from inside and outside the White House began to come crashing down on Nixon. Top White House assistants to the president, H.R. Haldeman and John Ehrlichman, as well as John Dean, Nixon's White House counsel, resigned under a cloud of suspicion on April 30, 1973. Then Attorney General Richard Kleindienst resigned. Days later Nixon, fighting for damage control, went before the U.S. people on television and assured them: "I am not a crook."

"What Did the President Know?"

More testified concerning their roles in the Watergate break-in. One of those was John Dean, who directed accusations concerning Nixon to the Ervin committee. Dean first opened his testimony by reading a 245-page statement, which took an entire day, even as the major television networks provided wall-to-wall coverage. It appeared that, while Nixon had not ordered the break-in at the Watergate offices or even known of the plan to burglarize Democrat headquarters, he had participated in a cover-up after the fact. Such damaging testimony led Senate committee member, Republican Howard Baker of Tennessee, to ask the question: "What did the president know and when did he know it?"

Even as Nixon accepted repeated resignations from White House officials, he insisted that he himself had had nothing to do with the Watergate burglary. In mid-summer Haldeman and Ehrlichman appeared before the Senate committee and claimed that John Dean had been the mastermind behind the White House cover-up of the break-in. Their story might have stuck if former White House deputy chief of staff, Alexander P. Butterfield, had not testified on July 16 that Nixon had installed a tape-recording system in the White House's Oval Office. Such tapes might prove Dean's guilt or innocence, not to mention that of President Nixon.

President Nixon's press secretary, Ron Ziegler, fields questions about the Watergate scandal at a press conference in Washington, D.C., in May 1973. Ziegler defended Nixon throughout the scandal.

Immediately the Ervin committee, along with Archibald Cox, a Harvard law professor who had been appointed by the White House as a special prosecutor for Watergate, requested the tapes from the president. When Nixon refused, claiming executive privilege, a titanic struggle began, one that continued over the next year. Nixon even ordered that Cox be fired, but Attorney General Elliot Richardson refused, choosing to resign instead as a matter of principal. Richardson's deputy, William Ruckelshaus, also resigned rather than fire Cox. Finally a third White House official, Solicitor General Robert Bork, fired Cox. Judge John Sirica recalled later, notes historian Allen Weinstein: "As I watched the story unfold on television, I couldn't get away from the feeling that the president had lost his grip on reality."

Adding to the cloud of scandal already hanging over the White House was the resignation on October 10, 1973, of Vice President Spiro Agnew over a completely unrelated case. (As Governor of Maryland, he had accepted bribes from construction company officials.) With Agnew's departure, Nixon selected Michigan congressman Gerald R. Ford as his vice president.

On November 1 a new special prosecutor was appointed, a Texan named Leon Jaworski, who had been a close associate of President Johnson. Over the months that followed, into the spring of 1974, Nixon fought to hang on to both his tapes and his presidency. He finally released full written versions of the tapes to Congress on April 29. What the tapes revealed was a scheming president, one who became consumed with secrecy and damage control.

Nixon Threatened with Impeachment

But the transcripts did not satisfy the House Judiciary Committee, which had taken up hearings of its own. Differences appeared between the text in the transcripts and a handful of tapes that the committee had in its possession. These included a curious 18-minute gap in the tape dated "June 20, 1972," only three days following the Watergate break-in. This raised further suspicions that Nixon was hiding something from Congress and the U.S. people. Two days after the release of the transcripts, the Judiciary Committee voted 20–18 to demand the full tapes. In the meantime, Special Prosecutor Jaworski was submitting subpoenas asking for the full tapes as well. When Nixon refused, claiming "national security," the committee voted 28–10 to inform the president that he was risking impeachment. Among those who voted against Nixon were several Republicans.

The Watergate affair had devolved into a standoff of legal issues, ultimately decided by the U.S. Supreme Court, which agreed to hear the case on May 31, 1974. This unique case, titled *United States v. Nixon*, ended with the unanimous decision that the president was required to turn over the Oval Office tapes to the Special Prosecutor. When Nixon delayed the turnover by several days, the House Judiciary Committee had reached the end of its rope, voting on July 27 to approve the first of three articles of impeachment—"impeding the administration of justice." With Republicans voting against Nixon, it appeared nearly certain that the president was bound for impeachment and that a Senate trial of Nixon would follow.

NIXON FORCED TO RESIGN

Then Judge John Sirica ordered Nixon's Special Counsel, James D. St. Clair, to listen to the tape dated June 23 to examine its content. This tape was the one dated closest to the Watergate break-in, given the June 20 partial erase. What St. Clair and several other White House officials heard was what prosecutors had been looking for over the previous year—direct evidence of Nixon's involvement in a cover-

PRESIDENT NIXON RESIGNS

On August 9, 1974, Nixon boarded a helicopter to leave the White House.

In his resignation speech, President Nixon stated: "*In all the decisions I have made in my public life, I have always tried to do what was best for the Nation. Throughout the long and difficult period of Watergate, I have felt it was my duty to persevere, to make every possible effort to complete the term of office to which you elected me. In the past few days, however, it has become evident to me that I no longer have a strong enough political base in the Congress to justify continuing that effort*".

up. The tape included the president in conversation with Haldeman, discussing the FBI's investigation of the break-in, including tracing the money found on the burglars. Haldeman informed Nixon that Attorney General John Mitchell had suggested that the president should instruct the CIA to order the Federal Bureau of Investigation (FBI) to halt its investigation and "stay the hell out of this." As the tape reels turned, St. Clair could hear Nixon agree to the plan, saying: "All right, fine." The June 23 tape provided prosecutors with their "smoking gun."

St. Clair had no choice but to insist on the release of the tape, as, after hearing the conversation and gaining knowledge of the cover-up, he was technically a part of the conspiracy. The tape was released on August 5. On the heels of the tape's release, seven Republican members of the House Judiciary Committee who had not voted against Nixon announced that they would now support impeachment. Having finally run out of options and with the integrity of his presidency in a shambles, Nixon went on television on August 8 and announced he would resign effective at noon the next day.

More than two years had passed since the bungled burglary at the Watergate complex. The illegal plan was designed to help reelect President Nixon. Some of the perpetrators had participated in the break-in at Democratic Party headquarters. Others and those within the White House who had dispatched them into the night to plant bugs in rotary telephones likely had never envisioned that their illegal plans, would lead to his, and their, ultimate downfall.

4

Ford and Carter

For nearly two years the nation had watched as the Watergate scandal unfolded and the Nixon administration finally burst apart at the seams. Following the first presidential resignation in U.S. history, a new chief executive entered the White House. For the first time a president came to power without having been elected either president or vice president. Gerald Ford had been hand-appointed by Nixon as his vice president following the resignation a year earlier of Vice President Spiro Agnew. Prior to his appointment Ford had served as the minority leader in the House.

When Ford became the nation's thirty-eighth president, Americans were prepared to put the drama of Watergate behind them. While the scandals had badly tarnished the office of the president, Watergate had also revealed how resilient the nation's institutions were, including Congress, the court system, even the press. Each had met the challenge of a president who acted as though he was above the law.

Even though Nixon had resigned, the former president was still liable for his crimes and could have faced criminal charges. Ford had earlier stated that he did not intend to pardon Nixon, but just a month after the departed president's resignation, the new president issued a pardon, telling the U.S. people at his inauguration: "My fellow Americans, our long national nightmare is over." The pardon angered some Americans, who thought Nixon had not been punished enough by simply resigning. Despite Ford's best intentions, some believed the pardon represented a deal made between Nixon and his successor, but no evidence of such an agreement has ever come to light.

Congress, though, in an effort to limit executive power, had already passed the War Powers Act (1973) which required future chief executives to confer with Congress before taking significant military action, set limits on campaign contributions, and beefed up the 1966 Freedom of Information Act, which placed the burden of proof on government entities, including the White House, to justify classifying information as secret or vital to maintaining national security.

FORD AT THE WHEEL

At his core, Gerald Ford was an honest, likeable individual who enjoyed a generally high level of popular support in the wake of the Nixon years. A former college football player, Ford was seen as a simple, even ordinary, guy. However, within three weeks of each other during the fall of 1975, there were two attempts to assassinate Ford, and both by women—Lynette Fromme and Sara Jane Moore. Fromme's attempt was foiled when a Secret Service agent grabbed her handgun before she fired. Moore's action failed as her first shot narrowly missed and her second shot was deflected when a bystander grabbed her arm as she fired.

Yet his inability to come to grips with national problems, such as the recession, caused Ford to lose support fairly early in his administration. His pardon of Nixon alone caused his approval rating to drop from 72 to 49 percent.

THE WOMEN'S LIBERATION MOVEMENT

During the early 1970s a movement to alter the roles of women in America was reaching millions eager for change. Sometimes called the Women's Liberation Movement, its leaders called for changes in the perception of women, including attitudes and prejudices that assumed women should remain at home and raise children, while only participating in the workforce in limited roles.

The movement's roots may well have extended back to the early nineteenth century and the efforts of such women's rights advocates as Elizabeth Cady Stanton and Susan B. Anthony. But the modern movement had evolved out of the 1960s, a time when female writers and academics were reconsidering the traditional roles for women. Betty Friedan's book, *The Feminine Mystique* (1963) was one of the first to question whether all women might find satisfaction in their roles as housewives. By 1966 Friedan had become one of the founders of the National Organization for Women (NOW).

While some of the new feminists railed loudly against "male chauvinism," which blamed men for keeping women in their traditional places, others pursued their individual goals without extreme political expression. One significant social change brought about by the women's movement was a change of course nationally regarding a woman's right to an abortion. In 1973 the U.S. Supreme Court handed down the *Roe v. Wade* decision, which legalized abortion in America. The women's rights movement also led Congress to pass the Equal Rights Amendment in 1972, which was designed to eliminate discrimination against women, but the amendment was never ratified.

Ford was, by political nature, a conservative, a leader who believed in less government. This led him to veto more than 60 bills during his tenure as president—besting fellow Republican Herbert Hoover's record in half the time.

Despite Ford's best intentions, the nation's economic health continued to slide during his two years in office. By 1975 Americans were struggling with the worst recession since the Great Depression, which included rising inflation and unemployment approaching 10 percent. Several important sectors of the economy, such as the automobile industry and construction, were in especially bad shape. By 1976 federal spending had reached a deficit level of $60 billion, a national record to date. Ford's answers for this economic crisis were too few and too ineffective. Preferring to steer clear of wage and price controls of the type Nixon had implemented, Ford seemed to do little else but establish a slogan against inflation, printed on red and white buttons that read "WIN," which stood for "Whip Inflation Now." Despite his conservative tendencies, Ford finally had to follow Congress's lead and accept a tax cut (one he had previously fought) in an effort to "prime the pump" to restart the nation's economy.

THE KISSINGER YEARS CONTINUE

One Nixon official who had remained unscathed by the Watergate scandal was his national security adviser, Henry Kissinger. Kissinger remained secretary of state during Ford's presidency, working to stabilize the Middle East, keeping up the administration's new relationship with China, and juggling détente with the Soviets. As Nixon had, President Ford met with Soviet leader Leonid Brezhnev, a relative Kremlin hardliner. In Vladivostok, Siberia, the two men worked out the structure for a new nuclear arms agreement—SALT II—in 1974. The following year the Soviets and Americans met during the summer in Helsinki, Finland, where the Russians made a pledge to recognize and respect human rights.

There were other, limited achievements in foreign policy during the Ford administration. Israel had captured and held the Sinai Peninsula following the Six Day War in 1967, but Kissinger now managed to get the Israelis to return this territory to the Egyptians. In addition, after two wars in less than a decade, Israel and Egypt agreed to concentrate on negotiating their differences with one another, rather than resorting to yet a third war.

The Vietnam War is Finished

But such successes for Ford and his administration became somewhat lost in 1975 with the end of the war in Vietnam. In early 1973 Kissinger had worked out a ceasefire in Vietnam, gaining an agreement from the North Vietnamese to halt their military efforts against South Vietnam. But by the spring of 1975 the North was again advancing toward Saigon, intent on gaining the final victory in Vietnam. This campaign had taken shape back in October 1974. At that time, the North had considered whether their actions would pull the United States back into the war. It would not.

In March 1975, as North Vietnamese troops moved across the Demilitarized Zone (DMZ) that divided the two Vietnams, Ford approached Congress for money and troops to be sent to Vietnam. (Nixon had tried the same thing the previous year.) But Congress was done with the war. When the legislators turned down Ford's request in late April, Ford read the handwriting on the wall, stating, notes historian Edward Ayers, that the Vietnam War "is finished as far as America is concerned."

The collapse of South Vietnam to Communist forces was paralleled by the fall of the governments of neighboring Cambodia and Laos that same spring. In some respects the old Cold War "domino theory" had come true. Another signal of the failure of U.S. efforts in Southeast Asia took place in May, when the takeover government of Cambodia, the ruthless Khmer Rouge, captured an unarmed U.S. merchant ship, the *Mayaguez*.

Desperate to make some show of force in the region, Ford ordered 2,000 U.S. marines to raid into Cambodia through U.S. ally Thailand and rescue the ship's crew. Ironically, the crew was released before the marines arrived, yet fighting broke out, resulting in the deaths of 40 military personnel. It was, perhaps, a well-intended effort by Ford, which many Americans applauded, thinking it represented to the world and to the many new governments in Southeast Asia that the United States was still a power with which to reckon.

THE "BICENTENNIAL ELECTION"

In 1976 the United States celebrated the 200th anniversary of the adoption of the Declaration of Independence. It was a year of looking back at U.S. history, and at the many paths the country had followed since separating from Great Britain and establishing the first democratic republic in the history of modern times. Patriotism was on display on a grand scale. That summer the July celebrations sizzled across the country, as fireworks and political speeches signaled America's past and its present. The nation's bicentennial was also an election year, and a struggling Gerald Ford was facing off with not only Democratic challengers, but with rivals from within the ranks of the Republicans.

Ford's greatest threat from within his own party came from a former governor of California, known more from his days as a film and television actor than from party politics—Ronald Reagan. Reagan delivered speeches in which he referred to Ford as a weak president, and just narrowly missed winning the Republican nomination. The Democrats were still nervous from the abject failure of the McGovern campaign, four years earlier. In 1976 almost a dozen Democrats stepped forward seeking the nomination, including longtime Massachusetts senator, Edward Kennedy, younger brother to John and Robert. But the party finally landed on a

During the Bicentennial Celebrations, Americans held parties to commemorate the struggle for independence, honoring patriotic heroes and displaying national icons.

previously little-known, one-term governor of Georgia and peanut farmer from the small town of Plains—James Earl Carter Jr., who went by the informal name "Jimmy." Carter labeled himself as a Washington outsider. It was a tactic that drew voters in; that, and his constant grin, his shirt-sleeve informality, and his promise that he would never lie to the U.S. people—a significant message in the age of Watergate.

Come November Carter slipped past Ford with 41 to 39 million votes, while garnering 297 electoral to Ford's 240. Crucial to the Southern Democrat's win was support from black Southern voters, as he captured every Southern state except for Virginia. But, unfortunately, the Watergate scandal may have soured many voters on the political process, as almost half of all eligible voters stayed away from the polls. As one car-bumper sticker read: "Don't vote. It only encourages them."

THE CARTER YEARS

At the outset of his presidency Jimmy Carter did represent, to many Americans, a breath of fresh politics in Washington. Carter was by nature an informal person, one who dressed in a cardigan sweater for his first presidential television address. On the road he was likely to carry his own suitcase. Like Ford, Carter was an honest individual, well-meaning, a strong Baptist, who represented a moral compass for the country in an era that seemed to lack moral clarity.

While the new president had been elected on the campaign drumbeat of selling himself as someone who was not a Washington politics kind of guy, he made a tactical error from his first days in office by remaining aloof with Congress while trying to micromanage his office. Carter was, as historian William E. Leuchtenburg notes, "politically insensitive and didn't know how to interact with the power brokers in Washington." Carter's chief of staff, Hamilton Jordan, also from Georgia, bragged that he never returned tele-phone calls from members of Congress. Carter remained a loner and a workaholic, who busied himself with mundane details, including approving who used the White House ten-nis courts and when.

The Carter administration was not without its early accom-plishments and symbolic steps forward. Carter appointed more blacks, Hispanics, and women to his administration than any previous president, and he created two new cabi-net positions, the Departments of Energy and of Education. Although controversial, he offered amnesty to thousands of young American men who had fled the country (typically to Canada) to avoid the draft and service in Vietnam. As Ford's pardon of Nixon had raised howls across the country, so this move did with many conservatives. Other changes included a serious stab at reforming the civil service, so that it would provide rewards for efficiency and productivity and protec-tion against political intrusion. Carter also pushed for vital environmental legislation, including a bill that would limit strip mining, and the creation of a "Superfund," which was expected to spend $1 billion a year in federal dollars to clean up toxic waste sites. Over the years there were more such sites to clean up than there was money, but the legislation represented, as historian James Patterson notes, "a signifi-cant environmental accomplishment of the Carter years."

Energy Issues

However, Carter soon faced many of the same problems that Ford (and Nixon before him) had wrestled with—and with no more success. The early achievements of his presidency would soon be overshadowed by the issue of the nation's economy. As energy issues seemed at the center of the nation's economic woes, Carter made new policy, by developing tax incentives (as well as penalties) to bolster energy conservation. He pushed for new oil and gas production at home, as well as the development of solar power and synthetic fuels. He gave tepid support to expanding the nation's reliance on nuclear power plants. (Halfway through his term, in March 1979, the nuclear reactor at Three Mile Island outside Harrisburg, Pennsylvania, malfunctioned, threatening to release radioactive fallout into the atmosphere. Although technicians contained the radiation, the mishap soured many on expanding nuclear facilities in America. Today nearly all of the country's 100 nuclear power plants still in service were built before the spring of 1979.)

Carter's energy plan, even when it passed in August 1978, was a shell of what he had originally presented. It included decontrolling natural gas prices and setting up tax credits for energy conservation. That summer, when renewed violence in the Middle East caused a shortage of oil imports, long lines at the gas pump were once again the norm. Then, between 1979 and 1980, OPEC doubled oil prices, causing a gallon (3.8 liters) of gasoline to hit $1 for the first time. In the meantime Carter's approval rating plummeted, reaching 26 percent before the end of 1979—lower than Nixon's had fallen in the darkest days of the Watergate crisis.

CARTER'S DIPLOMACY

The president, who came to the White House with no real foreign policy experience, brought together a mixed group of foreign policy team players. He chose Andrew Young, a civil rights leader, as his U.N. ambassador; Cyrus Vance, a longtime veteran of the State Department, as his secretary of state; and Polish-born Zbigniew Brzezinski, a professor at Columbia University, as his national security adviser. Sometimes these individuals failed to cooperate with one another and on occasions they presented conflicting advice to President Carter, who was left confused and uncertain about which direction to take in foreign matters. Unfortunately, this team was soon put to the test.

In efforts to improve relations with the Soviets and lessen the threat of nuclear war, Carter (with support from Vance) shut down production of the B-1 bomber, a plane intended to replace the aging B-52s used in Vietnam. He also canceled the development of the neutron bomb. In early 1979 the president established diplomatic relations with the People's Republic of China (Communist China), which, again, angered conservatives and further isolated Taiwan.

Interfering in South America

A strong supporter of human rights, Carter cut off U.S. support for the harsh leadership of Chile, and he cut ties with the repressive regime in Nicaragua of Anastasio Somoza Debayle, whose family had ruled the country since 1937. Some critics blamed Carter when, in July 1979, Marxist Sandinistas threw out Somoza and installed a Communist government. Carter also tried to push the leaders of Brazil and Argentina to further embrace democracy. He worked out a treaty with Panama to hand over the canal by the end of the century. This move, especially, met with conservative challenge, and the Senate ratified the treaty with only a single vote to spare. Voting for this treaty ultimately cost several congressional supporters their seats, as 20 senators were ousted at the polls either in 1978 or 1980.

Progress in the Middle East

Carter did manage one diplomatic coup during his presidency. He brought together the leaders of Israel and Egypt for face-to-face talks. In September 1978 Carter invited Israeli Prime Minister Menachem Begin and Egypt's President Anwar el-Sadat to come to the United States for two weeks of negotiations over the key issues dividing the two

Middle Eastern powers. The two powers had already nego-tiated between themselves, beginning in 1977 when the forward-looking Sadat broke with his Arab neighbors and visited Israel to talk of peace. But those talks had stalled, and Carter was intent on breathing new life into them.

The talks were held at Camp David, the presidential retreat. The agreement between the two Middle Eastern leaders called for Israel to return land in the Sinai to Egypt. In exchange, Egypt would recognize the right of Israel to exist—something no Arab leader had ever done. But the treaty did little to help the Palestinians, who had lost control of their homeland when Israel was created back in 1948. The Gaza Strip and the West Bank would remain in the hands of the Israelis.

REVOLUTION IN IRAN

But for all of the struggles of the Carter administration, none represented a greater difficulty for the president and the nation than the events that engulfed Iran in 1979. During the previous 25 years Iran had been ruled by Emperor Mohammed Reza Shah Pahlavi, a westernized leader who sought to modernize his nation and his people by bringing about a series of reforms. These included land redistribution, expanded industry, Western educations for young Iranian college students, and social reforms that included increased rights for women, such as liberalized divorce laws. The Shah was unpopular for his strong control of his country and the tactics of his secret police, and opposition now grew from fundamentalist Islamists. Revolution spread, until the Ira-nian ruler was ousted in January 1979.

During the months that followed, an ailing, extreme cler-ic, Ayatollah Ruhollah Khomeini, was brought out of exile in Paris and into power through a national referendum. He established a conservative Islamic republic as he preached anti-Westernism. By summer the Shah was ill with cancer and sought treatment in the United States. After Carter agreed to let the deposed Iranian leader come to New York for medical care, anti-American protests spread across Iran and Iranian "students" took control of the U.S. embassy in the capital, Tehran. Sixty-six Americans were taken hostage. In short order, 14 of them were released, leaving 52 in the hands of extremists. Despite U.S. protests, these captives remained hostages for 444 days, the remainder of Carter's term of office. News reports showed Iranian extremists parading blindfolded Americans in the streets of Tehran as bystanders burned U.S. flags.

The following month Carter faced another foreign policy crisis, when the Soviets invaded Iran's neighbor, Afghanistan. This country was in the throes of its own fundamentalist Muslim takeover, which was threatening the Communist government there. Carter seemed paralyzed by these events, and his public support simply collapsed. When diplomacy with Iran proved fruitless, he finally gave approval for a military rescue mission in April 1980. This failed miserably when a U.S. helicopter malfunctioned and crashed into a transport plane on the ground, killing eight U.S. commandos. Secretary Vance resigned in anger over the aborted mission. Carter's presidency was probably the ninth casualty that day.

5

The Reagan Revolution

So much of the politics of the 1970s played havoc with the psyche of the American people. The ragged decade had been punctuated by the collapse of South Vietnam, the cynicism of the Watergate scandal, the fall and resignation of a U.S. president, followed by two lackluster presidents, energy shortages, a crippled economy, and the national humiliation that was the Iranian Hostage Crisis. All this created in many Americans what Carter himself referred to as a "crisis of confidence." Nothing seemed reliable—the economy, the military, the political system, even America's future. By 1980 the United States seemed on the decline.

THE ELECTION OF 1980
Although most Americans no longer had any faith in Carter serving a second term, he managed to grab a nomination from the Democrats at their mid-August convention in New York City. The Republicans approached the campaign with

enthusiasm, rallying behind the contender who had almost taken the nomination from Ford back in 1976—Ronald Reagan. Many Americans knew Reagan from his days as a Hollywood actor. George Herbert Walker Bush, a veteran political figure in Washington, was tapped as Reagan's vice presidential running mate. Reagan planned to lower taxes, reduce the size of government, rebuild the nation's military, and stand firm against Communism. On another level, Reagan tapped into the hearts of many voters when he spoke of restoring U.S. vitality, strength, and pride.

On election day—which was, coincidentally, the first anniversary of the seizure of the U.S. hostages—Reagan won a stunning victory, gaining 51 percent of the vote. In addition the Republicans won control of the U.S. Senate for the first time since 1952. Democrats hung on to the majority of seats in the House, but the mood of the country was conservative and many in the House, both Republicans and Democrats, seemed onboard with Reagan. Inauguration day not only brought a new president to the White House, but also the release of the American hostages in Iran. Their 444-day nightmare finally had ended.

REAGAN'S POLITICAL IMPRINT

Reagan was poised in January 1981 to deliver more significant retooling and redefining of the role of government in the lives of Americans since the days of the New Deal half a century earlier. Some of Reagan's success was about having a forceful, human presence in the office of the presidency. He was a gifted speaker, who presented his goals in a straightforward, unadorned, and uncomplicated manner and with a personal ease that drew people in rather than turned them off. Even those who did not agree with Reagan's positions typically still liked him. When he was shot in March 1981 by a mentally disturbed young man named John Hinckley Jr., television reporters related how Reagan joked with his doctor on the way to surgery, "Are you a Republican?" to which the surgeon replied warmly: "Today, Mr. President, we are all Republicans."

During the twentieth century only five or so presidents have brought as much personality to the office as Reagan: both Roosevelts, Kennedy, and, later, Bill Clinton. Not a deep

President Ronald Reagan talks to Israeli Prime Minister Menachem Begin during his visit to Washington, D.C., on September 9, 1981. Israel was opposed to Reagan's sale of Airborne Warning and Control System (AWACS) aircraft to Saudi Arabia.

thinker, in the same way that Franklin Roosevelt was not, Reagan nevertheless managed to create a presidency that left an indelible mark on the U.S. social and political landscape.

CONSERVATIVE ECONOMICS

President Reagan wasted almost no time in implementing his broad-based plan to bring the nation's economy back to a healthy status. The Carter years had been devastating. Interest rates, unemployment, and inflation had all risen steadily. Reagan had his work cut out for him.

He would rely on "supply-side economics," which some critics dubbed "Reaganomics." According to this theory, the core problem with the U.S. economy was that high taxes were hindering investment capital. To Reagan, the solution was simple: lower taxes. This would lead to greater levels of investment, creating a stronger, expansive economic system. Within his first few months as president, Reagan constructed a package of legislation centered on his pivotal supply-side economics theory. His "Economic Recovery" bill proposed $40 billion in budget cuts and he managed to get nearly all of them through Congress. Reagan then pushed through a tax-cut bill, which called for reductions of up to 25 percent in personal and corporate taxes over the next three years.

At first it appeared that Reaganomics might not be the answer to the nation's economic malaise. In the spring of 1982 the country slipped into a deeper recession, the lowest level of the economy since the Great Depression of the 1930s. Yet the new downturn did not last long. By the following year supply-side did indeed seem to be turning things around. That summer unemployment was down, the gross national product had expanded, and inflation dipped. Suddenly, the economy was on the mend.

In achieving this turnaround, Reagan did benefit from additional factors that were not directly of his making. Carter and Ford had struggled with upward-creeping oil and other energy prices, but during Reagan's first term oil prices stabilized, and even dropped, due to a glut of oil on the market. This severely damaged OPEC's potential to manipulate the oil markets. Otherwise tight money policies encouraged the drop in inflation rates.

A Gap in the Plan

Reagan had tamed major sectors of the economy, but he did not manage to accomplish a balanced federal budget, which he had planned on achieving through reductions in the size and number of government programs. Despite his promise of balancing the national ledger by the end of his first term, Reagan instead oversaw the accumulation of record budget deficits. He racked up more debt during his eight-year presidency than the U.S. government had done over the previous two centuries. The deficits were so massive and so unpopular with many Americans that Reagan actually felt compelled by the middle of his second term to go to Congress and ask for tax increases.

Why had Reagan failed to reduce the size of the federal government as he had promised he would during his campaign? One of the most significant reasons was the cost of "entitlement" programs, such as Social Security and Medicare. Such programs were automatically funded each year and were considered by many in Congress as untouchable. Thus reducing the cost of these "big ticket" items in a given federal budget was impossible for Reagan to accomplish on his own. Another major factor was higher military spending: Reagan called for massive increases in the Pentagon's budget, amounting to $1.6 trillion over a five-year period.

Hampered from cutting federal spending by entitlements and increased military spending, Reagan had to take unpopular steps and reduce spending on "discretionary" domestic programs. These included cuts in food stamps, low-income housing subsidies, limits on Medicare and Medicaid payments, limits on educational programs, such as college student loans and school lunch programs, and less funding for the National Endowment for the Arts and Humanities. But Reagan could only go so far. By the end of 1983 Congress would agree to few such cuts.

"THE EVIL EMPIRE"

A lifelong opponent of Communism, Reagan backed an aggressive set of policies intended to limit its reach. He supported foreign nations who were friendly to the United States, while engaging in tough negotiations, as well as rhetoric, against the Soviet Union.

Almost immediately U.S.–Soviet relations went cold. In June 1982, in a speech to the British Parliament, Reagan promoted his plan to build up the number of missiles based in Europe. He talked of advancing democracy and destabilizing Communist states supported by the Soviet Union. At one point in his address, Reagan made his ultimate objective clear: "What I am describing now is a plan . . . which will leave Marxism-Leninism on the ash heap of history." The following year, speaking before a group of evangelical ministers in Florida, Reagan referred to the Soviet Union as an "evil empire."

But the president knew that words alone would not change anything. Action had to follow, and Reagan announced in 1983 his proposal for one of the most ambitious military programs in U.S. history, his Strategic Defense Initiative (SDI). Critics soon dubbed this "Star Wars," after the popular 1970s film. The plan was to launch satellites armed with lasers into orbit around the Earth, with the aim of "shooting down" incoming enemy nuclear-tipped missiles, thus rendering nuclear war (by missile) impossible and out-of-date.

A New Soviet Leader

While Star Wars is still being developed, the idea of a system of killer lasers in space capable of destroying Soviet missiles had the Russians extremely concerned. They insisted that the United States must stop pursuing this development before they would make any agreement on nuclear weapons. In

THE ELECTION OF 1984

While Reagan had won the 1980 election by a singular majority, his reelection in 1984 was not always assumed. Having taken bold steps to repair the nation's damaged economy, his first two years in office had not only failed to deliver a recovery, but brought on a worsening recession. For a while, Reaganomics seemed to have failed. But during the second half of his first term, the economy did finally improve dramatically. Reagan and the Republicans took the opportunity to claim responsibility for the new prosperity, and many Americans were prepared to let them. As Reagan had symbolized a new faith and patriotism in America, so people across the country now felt the nation was improving, thanks to the president.

The Democratic Party went with who they had: Walter Mondale, who had served as Jimmy Carter's vice president. Mondale understood that his campaign would be an uphill battle. He did receive backing from important national organizations, such as the NAACP, labor unions, and the National Organization of Women. He also took the calculated step of choosing a woman as his running mate—Geraldine Ferraro, a House member from New York.

At no point during the campaign did Mondale lead in the polls. In the minds of many Americans he simply could not be separated from the Carter administration that had failed to fix the economy, while Reagan represented to them successful strategies that had delivered a return of prosperity. On election day Ronald Reagan won all the states in the Union except the District of Columbia and Mondale's Minnesota.

1985 Reagan and the new leader of the Soviet Union, Mikhail Gorbachev, met in Geneva, Switzerland, for a summit. Gorbachev was ready to deliver significant reforms in the Soviet Union, and was interested in reaching an agreement with the West on nuclear weapons so that he could channel Soviet monies away from military spending and toward domestic problems. The next year Reagan and Gorbachev met in Iceland for two days of talks on reducing arms. At one point the two leaders seriously talked of banning nuclear weapons outright on both sides, but an impasse on SDI stood in the way. Following the Iceland summit both countries stepped back, keeping their talks to a minimum and focusing almost exclusively on taking out all short-range nuclear weapons in Europe. The two leaders did agree on the Intermediate-range Nuclear Forces (INF) Treaty in December 1987.

Gorbachev was not the typical Soviet premier. He had come to understand that the days of Soviet Communism were likely numbered, and that the future would bring times of extraordinary change for his country and for those East European nations that had chafed under Soviet control for more than 40 years. In 1988 he announced that he was cutting the Soviet military by 500,000 men and that he was set to pull out six Soviet armored divisions from East Germany, Czechoslovakia, and Hungary over the next two years. The Soviet Union was losing control of its own future.

THE IRAN–CONTRA SCANDAL

Even as Reagan engaged in thrust and parry tactics with the Soviets, his administration also tried to push back Communism in various places around the world. The president's policy became known as the Reagan Doctrine, and it saw activity in Grenada in October 1983 and later in the Central American nation of El Salvador, where Marxist Sandinista forces from Nicaragua were threatening to topple the government. To give support to the government of El Salvador, Reagan officials became involved in a scheme to deliver military support and monies to counter-revolutionary anti-Sandinista forces, usually called Contras, who were already battling the Marxist government in Nicaragua. In 1982 and 1983 early attempts to support the Contras were spurned by Congress. A 1984 amendment to a spending bill specifically barred the Pentagon and CIA from providing "military equipment, military training or advice, or other support for military activities, to any group or individual . . . for the purpose of overthrowing the government of Nicaragua." The law was renewed in 1985 into 1986.

Questionable Deals

Reagan administration officials were not deterred, however. Unknown to Congress, officials facilitated secret arms sales to Iran, which had been banned by law following the Iranian Hostage Crisis. Reagan approved the sales, in the hope that Iran would use its influence to help release several Americans being held individually by various Islamic terrorist groups in Lebanon. The first shipment to Iran was made in July 1985 and resulted in the release of one of seven known hostages. A second secret shipment was delivered in May 1986. Once this military hardware had been sold, Reagan officials had millions of dollars from covert activity and no place to put it. Then the suggestion was made by a National Security Council staffer, Lt. Col. Oliver North, that $12 million of the funds be sent secretly to support the Contras. Without Reagan's knowledge, the money was sent. But news of the transfer leaked out by late fall in 1986.

In November an angry Reagan appointed a three-man commission to investigate the matter. The hearings revealed that the aid to the Contras had been approved by three top officials. In all, 14 Reagan officials were indicted and convicted, but only one received a jail sentence. Throughout the various investigations and trials, no credible evidence ever surfaced that Reagan had engaged in any criminal activity. But a public image of Reagan had emerged of a president who did not pay close enough attention to things said during cabinet meetings, to the point of nodding off to sleep. Reagan had given his men too much free rein, and they had taken it.

On July 14, 1987, Lieutenant Colonel Oliver North testifies before the U.S. Senate Iran–Contra Committee on U.S. government involvement in shipping arms to Iran to raise money for Contra guerillas.

END OF THE REAGAN ERA

The Iran–Contra scandal was just the worst of several black eyes the Reagan administration received in the last two years of his second term. Officials in the Environmental Protection Agency had to resign due to their mishandling of funds. One of Reagan's aides was convicted of perjury. His secretary of labor was indicted for fraud and resigned in disgrace. [He was later fully vindicated.] His attorney general was investigated for alleged wrongdoing and his secretary of housing and urban development also fell under investigation for impropriety in his distribution of housing grants.

In 1987 the economy took several dives, including the collapse of several savings and loan companies, a drop in the real estate market, and a serious collapse of the stock market on October 19, 1987, when there was a one-day drop of 508 points, the greatest single day freefall in the history of the market.

Nevertheless, Reagan and his aides continued to carry out their tasks to the end of his tenure of office. In 1988 new economic legislation made its way through Congress, including eliminating income taxes for low-income Americans, redefining capital gains as income, a dropping of the corporate tax rate, and a filling in of loopholes in the tax code. In August that year Congress passed the Japanese–American Reparations Act, which provided $20,000 to each Japanese-American who had been placed in a World War II-era relocation camp.

Reagan's Legacy

Despite serious blunders and shortfalls, when Reagan's presidency ended, the former Hollywood actor left a significant legacy. He had overseen a long-term economic recovery, helping to pull the country out of severe economic doldrums. He had given a new life to the U.S. military, while helping to develop new weapons systems aimed to take the nation's defense systems into the twenty-first century. He had also placed great pressures on the Soviet Union and Communism worldwide. And, perhaps as important as any other part of his legacy, Ronald Reagan, in his old-fashioned way, had restored patriotism in the minds of many Americans, giving them hope for their own future and that of their country.

That hope was something he carried through his life, his presidency, and his years of retirement. Reagan made his last significant public appearance in 1994 when he and four other presidents—Ford, Carter, George H. W. Bush, and Clinton—attended the funeral of Richard Nixon in California. By that time Reagan had been diagnosed with Alzheimer's Disease. Before year's end he sat down and penned a farewell letter to the people of the United States, in which he included the heart-felt words: "I now begin the journey that will lead me into the sunset of my life. I know that for America there will always be a bright dawn ahead."

6

Bush: The Last Cold Warrior

espite the successes of the Reagan administration, scandal had marred the last couple of years of his second term, leading the Democrats to believe that they had a good shot at winning back the White House in 1988. Michael Dukakis, Governor of Massachusetts, won the nomination in July at the Democratic National Convention in Atlanta. Vice President George Herbert Walker Bush received his party's nomination. Bush kept a strong lead throughout the campaign that fall and won the election with 48.9 million votes to his Democratic rival's 41.8 million. Electorally, Bush grabbed 426 votes and 40 states while Dukakis racked up only 111 votes from 10 states.

BUSH IN THE WHITE HOUSE

Born into a well-established Connecticut family, Bush had served in World War II, attended Yale University, and made a fortune in the oil business. In 1966 and again in 1968 he won a seat in the House of Representatives. The new president had an impressive political resume: He had served as ambassador to China and to the United Nations, and director of the CIA before being tapped as Reagan's vice president.

As president, Bush continued many of Reagan's economic policies. In 1989 he had to focus on the collapse of the savings and loan industry. The price tag for bailing out the affected savings and loans would stack up nearly a half trillion dollars. This only increased the national debt, which had already piled up to $2.6 trillion by the time Bush entered office. During his campaign, Bush had promised the U.S. public that he would not increase taxes. However, the deficit remained a looming statistic during his administration, and by 1990, he had become convinced that new taxes were necessary. In October Congress passed both tax hikes and spending cuts, designed to cut the budget deficit by a third of a trillion by the mid-1990s.

Bush sometimes lined himself up with Democratic Party goals. He supported the passage of the Clean Air Act, and in 1990 he signed legislation creating the Americans with Disabilities Act. The act was designed to fight discrimination against those who were physically or mentally disadvantaged.

THE END OF THE COLD WAR

President Bush brought extraordinary experience in foreign policy to his administration, and his most significant contributions as chief executive were in foreign affairs. In 1989 the Soviet Union seemed to implode. Gorbachev had set the stage through his policies of *perestroika* (retooling the socio-economic structure of the state) and *glasnost* (a transparency or openness within the USSR that opened the door for dissent). He had equally opened up his foreign policy to the Western powers, including the United States, in an effort to bring stability through trade and a decreased reliance on his nation's military and its costs.

Now the dominoes began to fall in rapid order. The Soviets pulled out of their disastrous war in Afghanistan. Gorbachev stated the Soviet Union had no right to interfere in Communist states and their internal affairs. Eastern bloc nations, which had been under the thumb of Soviet domination since the latter days of World War II, suddenly found the opportunity to break away, beginning first with Poland, then Hungary, Czechoslovakia, and Bulgaria. Only in Romania did the revolution against Communist control result in bloody violence. To old Cold War veterans, it all seemed surreal.

Then on November 9 came the fall of a longstanding symbol of Communist repression—the Berlin Wall. People on both sides of the wall wielded sledgehammers, pick axes, and even heavy equipment, to literally break through the wall that had divided Berlin since 1962. The Brandenburg Gate—"Checkpoint Charlie" to the West—was opened. People danced on top of the wall. On October 3, 1990, East Germany rejoined West Germany. The new Germany was pro-Western, continuing in NATO as the old Warsaw Pact collapsed. Soviet states, including Lithuania, Latvia, and Estonia, now demanded their freedom, followed by independence movements in other breakaway republics, including Uzbekistan, Ukraine, Georgia, Azerbaijan, and Armenia.

Such change in the Soviet Union meant that Gorbachev could negotiate with President Bush as never before. In 1990 the two leaders worked out a dozen agreements—reducing long-range nuclear warheads, stopping production of chemical weapons, and opening up new levels of trade between the two powers. Yet, for all his efforts, Gorbachev met strong opposition from Communist hardliners. A coup attempt was quashed. In December 1991, the ill Gorbachev stepped down

Germans celebrate their freedom to pass between East and West Germany as the Berlin Wall falls in November 1989. Removal of the wall paved the way for the reunification of Germany 11 months later.

as president. In the first free elections in recent Russian history, Boris Yeltsin was elected as the nation's new leader. By year's end, the old Soviet Union had morphed into the Commonwealth of Independent States, which included a dozen free and independent republics.

New agreements were made between the United States and the new Russian government led by Yeltsin. Bush announced that the U.S. military would dismantle its nuclear arsenals in Europe and Asia, while entering new talks with the Russians over cutting ICBMs. On the Russian side, similar cutbacks were promised. To the U.S. leader, the possibility of a Soviet invasion into Western Europe was so remote that it was considered "no longer a realistic threat." After years of continuous antagonism and animosity between the Soviets and the United States, Chairman of the Joint Chiefs of Staff, General Colin Powell, noted the Cold War "has vaporized before our eyes."

Movements for Democracy

Around the world, Communism seemed on the run, and democracy was pushed forward as the new political order of the day. After years of revolution and strife Nicaragua held free elections in February 1990 and removed the Sandinistas. In South America longtime Chilean leader, Augusto Pinochet, who had come to power through a bloody 1973 coup, allowed free presidential elections in 1989 and lost. In South Africa the age-old racial policies of apartheid were challenged by a new, white prime minister, Frederik W. de Klerk, who came to office in 1989, freed black nationalist Nelson Mandela the following year (Mandela had been a political prisoner for 27 years), and then began dismantling apartheid. In 1992, with support from de Klerk, blacks were beginning to experience full participation in the South African political process.

However, not all democratic movements succeeded. In Communist China in the spring of 1989, a student-led movement in support of democracy spilled out into the streets of Beijing. The protests centered in Tiananmen Square, where a crudely built, 30-foot (10-meter)-high statue of the "Goddess of Freedom," patterned after the Statue of Liberty, was symbolically paraded through the city. But, unlike the Soviet Union, the Chinese government was not on the brink of collapse, and officials ordered out tanks and machine guns against defiant protesters. Hundreds of young counter-revolutionaries were gunned down or imprisoned and executed after public trials were staged. The new breezes of freedom were unable to destroy repression everywhere. But much of the Cold War had finally reached its dramatic conclusion.

SADDAM INVADES KUWAIT

Even as the Soviet Union was unraveling and Communism in Eastern Europe appeared to have had its day, President Bush faced new crises in other parts of the world. In the Western Hemisphere General Manuel Noriega, who had been in power in Panama since 1983, was indicted in the United States for his involvement in the international drug trade. Bush dispatched 24,000 troops to Panama in late December as Operation Just Cause, but Noriega seemed to have disappeared. He surfaced in the Vatican embassy on Christmas Eve. After a week of negotiations Noriega surrendered. The operation resulted in the deaths of 23 U.S. troops and thousands of Panamanians, including civilians. Over the next year, Noriega was held in a U.S. federal jail. He was convicted in 1992 of racketeering and drug distribution.

On August 2, 1990, new trouble started in the Middle East as Iraqi dictator Saddam Hussein invaded neighboring, oil-rich Kuwait. Saddam had held power for more than a decade and had been at war with Iran during the 1980s.

As Iran and the United States had fallen into conflict, U.S. support for Iraq's efforts had seemed the right strategy at the time, so between 1985 and 1990 the United States had delivered half a billion in military and technological aid to Iraq. The Iran–Iraq War had ended in 1988 under a U.N. truce. In the aftermath Kuwait had increased its production of oil, despite an OPEC agreement to cut back. As oil prices dropped, Saddam, whose country relied entirely on oil production for its income, insisted that Kuwait must reduce its production. When Kuwait refused, Saddam took steps to invade his neighbor, despite strong words from the United States that it considered Kuwait vital to its own interests.

Rarely has a leader miscalculated the world's response to his actions so dramatically. Immediately the U.N. Security Council condemned the Iraqi invasion, by a vote of 14–0, followed by an embargo on trade with Iraq. U.S. and Soviet officials issued a joint statement against the military actions. Within the week U.S. and British military forces were dispatched to Saudi Arabia, a U.S. ally.

On November 29 the U.N. approved the use of force to remove Iraq from Kuwaiti soil. A date for Saddam's withdrawal was set at January 15, 1991. By year's end Bush had sent 500,000 U.S. troops into the Middle East.

THE PERSIAN GULF WAR

When several peace delegations to Iraq failed, Congress finally passed an additional resolution sanctioning U.S. military action on January 10, just five days before the U.N. deadline for Saddam's withdrawal. Already President Bush had pulled together an international force of 28 allied nations, including some of Saddam's own Arab neighbors, and preparations were underway for "Operation Desert Storm." That campaign opened on January 17 at 2:30 A.M. (Baghdad time) when the first missiles and planes were launched to strike against Iraqi targets. Although Saddam Hussein had promised the "mother of all battles," the Persian Gulf War was short and successful for the U.S. and Coalition forces. Saddam was not equipped to meet the challenge of an invasion force that included hundreds of thousands of troops. He soon fell into a fruitless strategy of launching Soviet-built Scud missiles, which were largely inaccurate, at Israel. He hoped that the Israelis would be provoked to attack, which might bring about a split in Bush's coalition, especially among his Arab allies. Meanwhile an invasion force of 200,000 troops—largely comprised of Americans, plus British and French troops—easily liberated Kuwait, after outflanking Saddam's "elite" Republican Guard by slipping through Saudi Arabia and then directly into Iraq.

The basic strategy of the allied effort had been developed by General Colin Powell, the chair of the Joint Chiefs of Staff, and carried out by field commander, General Norman Schwarzkopf, who soon became known as "Stormin' Norman." Americans were able to see footage of the war on television. Repeated replays of bombings through night vision technology gave the war the look of a deadly video game.

Overcome but Not Defeated

Saddam's forces were unable to match the inroads made by advanced U.S. tanks. The ground attack into Iraq began on February 24 and was completed just four days later. Thousands of Iraqi troops surrendered and, by February 28, President Bush called for a ceasefire. Three days earlier, Saddam had agreed to pull his forces out of Kuwait and to accept Kuwaiti independence.

Bush allowed Saddam to remain in power. At the time this decision seemed wise. Allied forces had already occupied 20 percent of Iraq and had inflicted 100,000 fatalities on Iraqi military and civilian personnel. U.S. fatalities only stood at fewer than 150. Rarely in history had U.S. forces accomplished so much in so little time with such limited casualties. The Persian Gulf War appeared to have ended successfully, but Saddam Hussein would continue to be a thorn in the side of the United States during the following decade.

Following Operation Desert Storm in January 1991, a destroyed Iraqi T-55 main battletank, painted with graffiti by Coalition troops, lies among other destroyed vehicles along the highway between Kuwait City and Basra, Iraq.

AN ALTERED SOCIAL FABRIC

Although foreign policy issues dominated the president's days, the changing social fabric of America also directly involved the Bush White House. The administration targeted illegal drug abuse as an important social cause when it was learned that more than a third of a million babies were

A NEW DISEASE

By the early 1990s a new disease was spreading across the country, one that seemed to target specific groups of people. It was called Acquired Immune Deficiency Syndrome, or AIDS. It was caused by the human immunodeficiency virus (HIV). The disease had first spread, it appears, in pockets of the country's gay community. By the summer of 1991 AIDS had already claimed the lives of more than 100,000 Americans, while an estimated 1.5 million were HIV-positive, meaning they were infected with the virus. Nine out of ten carriers were men, many of them homosexuals. Other groups significantly affected were blacks and Hispanics, as well as drug users, who spread the disease by sharing needles.

By 2000 the number of women infected had risen statistically, and AIDS research began in earnest.

Scientists searched for a cure or effective treatment, but, while drugs were developed to slow the disease's symptoms, no cure was forthcoming. Private groups and government-sponsored campaigns strove to enlighten Americans about a disease that was often misunderstood, including incorrect theories about how the disease might be contracted. Initial misinformation told how one might contract AIDS through casual kissing or from sitting on an "infected" toilet seat. Over the years, through education, the public came to understand the disease better, including ways of protecting themselves. Since AIDS was contracted primarily through sexual activity, some advocated "safe sex," including the use of condoms, while others encouraged abstinence programs.

born with cocaine or heroin addictions in 1989 alone. William J. Bennett, a former education secretary, was appointed as the head of the newly established Office of National Drug Control Policy, and was often known as the "Drug Czar." Such strategies as workplace drug testing, stricter law enforcement, and attempts to work with the governments of Colombia and Peru—source nations for drugs such as cocaine—had mixed results, including a 20 percent increase in drug-related arrests.

As government officials studied the reasons behind such rampant drug use, they associated the increase with a rising level of poverty. In 1992 the nation's poor included 10 percent of whites, 26 percent of Hispanics, and 30 percent of blacks. Among these groups, many were drop-outs from school. One statistic was that 40 percent of black male high school drop-outs were chronically unemployed. Despite the billions that had been spent by the government since the 1960s on better training, better schools, and better housing, the march of poverty in America was far from at an end.

The New Conservatives

Such problems needed solutions, but many Americans were unprepared or unwilling to take any overt actions on behalf of the poor or others struggling with unemployment or poor living conditions. Reagan had given a dramatic boost to the causes of conservatism in America during his presidency, and an era of political conservatism now took shape. Liberal issues, such as affirmative action, were assaulted from the right. Such programs had been designed to correct patterns of injustice by providing opportunities for historically oppressed minorities, but conservatives saw the pendulum swinging against them to the point that some minorities received preferential treatment at the expense of opportunities for whites.

To the far right of the new conservatives were such televangelist leaders as Jerry Falwell and Pat Robertson, whose organizations attempted to pressure politicians to support conservative stances, such as prayer in public schools and opposition to abortion. The number of conservative evangelicals in America had increased seven times over since the end of World War II, and many of them stood united against what they perceived as an age of immorality, with high drug use, dramatic increases in adolescent sexual activity, acceptance of gay rights, and the legalizing of abortion. Such changes in the social fabric upset those who believed in what they called "traditional family values."

THE 1990 CENSUS

In the midst of Bush's term as president, the federal government carried out the national census. This census revealed tremendous changes in America in relation to race, gender, and age. Through the 1980s the U.S. population had grown by 10 percent to nearly 250 million people. The nation had aged as the "baby boomers" grew older, shifting the median age from 30 to 33. The fastest growing group was older Americans. Thanks to medical advances, the number of people in their nineties had doubled over the previous 10 years and the number of centenarians had increased by 77 percent.

The nation's "Sunbelt" witnessed tremendous population growth, as many Americans packed up and moved south and west, causing declines in populations of such regions as the Northeast. These changes in national demographics meant that representation in Congress shifted, with Florida, California, and Texas gaining House seats, while such states as New York lost seats. Many of those who had moved during the 1980s had moved to the cities. Nine out of ten Americans had settled in large metropolitan centers, creating an increase in the number of urban centers in the country. For the first time in U.S. history, the majority of Americans were living in urban areas of 1 million people or greater. All this meant that the number of rural dwellers had dropped. The census showed that fewer than 5 million people—just 2 percent of the nation's entire population—lived on farms.

A multiracial class of students at a high school in Los Angeles. During the 1980s and early 1990s schools across the country experienced an influx of immigrants from Mexico and overseas.

The Changing Family

The census also revealed what many Americans already knew regarding the structure of the nation's families. Women had entered the U.S. workforce in record numbers. The workforce had grown, and 60 percent of the extra workers were women. These women were also breaking into job categories previously dominated by men: They comprised one-third of the new doctors, 23 percent of the new dentists, and 40 percent of the new lawyers.

A new demographic was a shift in the traditional family. Two-parent families—those in which both parents lived in the same household—dropped from 31 percent of all families in 1980 to 26 percent in 1990. For blacks, the shift was dramatic. In 1960 two out of every three black families had included a mother and father at home. Thirty years later this figure had dropped to fewer than two in five. There were other significant shifts, as well. A quarter of all homes consisted of one person living alone, in part due to young people postponing marriage and to the increase in the percentage of marriages that ended in divorce.

The Racial Mix

The 1990 census revealed that 25 percent of Americans were non-white. Blacks constituted 12 percent of the total population, while Hispanics came in at 9 percent, Asians at 3 percent, and American Indians at 1 percent. Growth rates among these races collectively had increased to twice what they had been prior to the 1970s. One factor responsible for the shift was an increase in legal immigration during the 1980s. In that single decade 7 million immigrants had taken residence in the United States, an increase of 30 percent over the 1970s, and higher than any other decade in the twentieth century except the first one, from 1901 to 1910. During the first six years of the 1990s an additional 6 million immigrants came to America, many from Mexico and Asia. These figures do not include the number of illegal aliens.

Some of these immigration trends revealed significant pockets of change across the country. Two out of every three Asians lived in California, along with one of every three Hispanics. Los Angeles became home to 2 million Mexican-Americans, making the southern California city the largest home to people of Mexican descent after Mexico City. Such cities as Miami, Florida, and San Antonio, Texas, now saw majorities of Hispanics in their populations, with 64 and 55 percent respectively.

7

The Clinton White House

In early 1991 Bush's handling of the Persian Gulf War caused his approval ratings at home to skyrocket. Democrats, looking to the following year and the presidential election, wondered if they had a ghost of a chance of getting a candidate elected. But during the 20 months between the end of the war and the election, Bush made significant stumbles. He threatened to veto civil rights legislation designed to simplify how an employee might "prove" discrimination on the part of his or her employer. (Later in 1991, he did sign a watery version.) He nominated a conservative black jurist, Clarence Thomas, to replace the first black justice on the Supreme Court, the liberal-minded Thurgood Marshall, who had died. A host of liberal groups, including the NAACP, opposed Thomas's nomination, but a Senate vote of 52–48 overrode such oppositions.

Capping off Bush's missteps was his handling of the economy. Unemployment stood at 7 percent by 1992, and the federal budget deficit hit $250 billion every year Bush was in the White House. Although he had promised during the 1988 campaign, "Read my lips, no new taxes," this proved a promise he was forced to abandon. He submitted a budget as early as 1990 that included $133 billion in new taxes. By 1992 the Democrats were a little more confident that they had a shot at the White House.

THE 1992 ELECTION

After a scrappy run through the primaries that spring, the Governor of Arkansas emerged as the Democratic Party's front-runner. William Jefferson Clinton, known as Bill Clinton, was forced to dodge accusations from within his own party of being a womanizer and evading the draft during the Vietnam War. But Americans seemed to like his political passion, and he proved potentially popular with black voters. He spoke of the Democratic Party having spent too many years in the wilderness, and said that it was time for its members to reclaim their legacy of being socially responsive to the needs of the U.S. people. Overhauling the nation's healthcare system appeared to be among his priorities. When nominated, Clinton chose a fellow Southerner, Senator Albert Gore from Tennessee, as his vice presidential running mate.

The Republicans stayed with Bush, but despite his clear successes, especially his leadership during the Persian Gulf War, he ran a lackluster campaign. Bush may have had a front row seat to the collapse of the Soviet Union and may have made his own small contributions, but in 1992 the nation was interested in better economic times. As Clinton's campaign strategist, James Carville, said: "It's the economy, stupid." One Democrat poster read: "Saddam Hussein Still Has His Job. Do you?" Complicating matters for Bush was the presence of a third party candidate, billionaire Texan H. Ross Perot. Perot probably pulled more votes away from

Bush than from Clinton and may have spoiled the election for the Republicans.

Clinton won the election, with nearly 45 million votes to Bush's 39.1 million. The electoral vote was telling, with Clinton taking 370 while Bush tallied just 168. Perot had a great showing for a third party candidate with nearly 20 million votes, the best result for a third party since Theodore Roos-

Democrat president-elect Bill Clinton and his wife, Hillary Rodham Clinton, celebrate on election night in 1992 after defeating President George Bush. Clinton became the nation's forty-second president.

evelt in the 1912 election. The Democrats also took control of both houses of Congress, with new members including 39 blacks, 19 Hispanics, 7 Asians, 1 American Indian, and 48 women. (During his first full year in office, Clinton also appointed a woman to the Supreme Court. Ruth Bader Ginsburg was the second woman in the court's history. The first, Sandra Day O'Connor, had been nominated by Ronald Reagan.) Bush may have been a World War II hero while Clinton was just a youngish Baby Boomer, but the people were disenchanted with Bush and enamored with Bill.

AWKWARD OPENINGS

Having gained 43 percent of the vote, Clinton misinterpreted his mandate and took several steps that revealed his overreaching. When he called for an open recruitment policy of homosexuals into the U.S. military, opposition was strong. The result was a compromise of "don't ask, don't tell," which meant that gays could serve in the military, but that they must not reveal their true sexual orientation. One of Clinton's first major losses was his attempt to "reform" the nation's healthcare system. One problem was that many Americans did not favor a major shift in the government's role in healthcare delivery. His second problem was that he placed his wife, First Lady Hillary Rodham Clinton, in charge of the task force empowered to redesign the healthcare system. Her secret meetings and extraordinarily complicated system did not pass the vote in Congress.

There were other missteps. In 1993 Clinton saw through the passage of the North American Free Trade Agreement (NAFTA), which established a free-trade zone between Mexico, the United States, and Canada. Opponents believed the new law would cause Americans to lose their jobs to low-paid Mexican workers. Clinton's support for NAFTA thus lost him some points with organized labor, which traditionally supported the Democrats. But NAFTA turned out to increase the competitiveness of the three countries in the global marketplace, and it is still in force today.

Guns and Violence

President Clinton did have successes during his first term, including seeing through Congress the "Brady Bill" in 1993, which established new gun control laws. He also saw passage in 1994 of a major anticrime bill, which banned some types of assault weapons. In 2004, however, this law lapsed, and the following administration did not push for its revival.

Meanwhile guns and violence made the headlines across the country during the 1990s. In April 1993 there was a standoff outside Waco, Texas, when the FBI tried to close down a religious commune run by the Branch Davidians for alleged weapons violations, child abuse, and false imprisonment. A bungled operation led to the compound being consumed by fire and resulted in the deaths of 77 members of the commune, including several women and children. Immediately Clinton and Janet Reno, his attorney general (the first female AG in U.S. history) took responsibility for the outcome of the raid.

In April 1995, on the second anniversary of the Waco siege, a domestic terrorist group led by Timothy McVeigh and Terry Nichols blew up a truck bomb outside a federal office building in Oklahoma City. The bombing killed 168 people, including 19 children at the facility's day care center. McVeigh was convicted on 11 counts for the bombing and executed by lethal injection in 2001, the first execution by the federal government in nearly 40 years.

While the Oklahoma bombers were extremist white Americans, Muslim terrorists also targeted Americans in 1993 by detonating bombs at the World Trade Center in New York City. A half dozen people were killed. This event would later seem insignificant by comparison to the attack against the Twin Towers in 2001, which ended in their destruction and the deaths of thousands.

CLINTON AND THE ECONOMY

By the mid-term elections in 1994, the U.S. electorate had become disenchanted with Democrat leadership. Hillary Clinton's mishandling of healthcare reform, and Congress's failure to repair it, convinced an increasingly conservative group of voters that the time was right for political change in Washington. The Republicans gained significant ground during the election, as the Democrats lost 52 seats in the House with no loss of Republican seats. Even the Democratic speaker of the House, Thomas Foley, failed to be reelected. This marked the first time a standing speaker had lost a re-election since 1862.

With the House now under Republican control, its new speaker, Newt Gingrich, was ready to implement his party's "Contract with America," which had been unveiled during the fall campaigns. At the heart of this contract was a promise by the Republicans to clean up the House and rid it of corruption. (In 1994, the American people had been disgusted by several House scandals, including sexual harassment and embezzlement through the Congressional Post Office.) However, while much of the agenda under the "Contract for America" passed through the House, including a bill to pass a constitutional amendment limiting House members' terms, the Senate prevented most of the changes from becoming reality.

Another of Gingrich's goals was to balance the federal budget. This did see the light of day, resulting in $1 trillion in federal budget cuts. To that end, the Speaker pushed the Democrats and Clinton to the wall by threatening to "shut down the government" if adequate budget cuts were not forthcoming. A face-off ensued in 1995, with funding for several federal government offices and programs running out by mid-November. Although vital services continued, many federal operations were closed, including the National Gallery of Art in Washington and national parks such as Grand Canyon, Yellowstone, and the Smoky Mountains.

Ultimately Clinton was forced to compromise with the Republicans on such measures. An astute political animal, the president could read the direction the country wanted to go. One of the significant program changes he supported was the Welfare Reform Bill of 1996, which cut deeply

AMERICA GOES ONLINE

By the mid-1990s a new technology was sweeping the United States as millions of Americans went "online." Although the interlinking system known as the Internet dated back to some pioneering efforts during the late 1960s, the World Wide Web did not become commonplace until the Clinton era.

The trend toward home computers began in 1981, when International Business Machines (IBM) announced to the public that it would begin marketing the new technology. Sales took off. By January 1983 sales of PCs (personal computers) had increased from 20,000 annually to more than 500,000. Home computing became commonplace by the late 1980s and early 1990s.

In 1996, 18 million Americans—roughly 9 percent of the population—had regular access to the Internet, either at work, at home, or both. A year later the number had already increased to 30 million. Today the Internet is available to the vast majority of Americans and for some the system has become their primary source for news, information, research, entertainment, and social networking. By the early 2000s such interactive social sites as Facebook and MySpace allowed Americans to stay in touch with one another and with others around the world.

into welfare payments while expecting able-bodied welfare recipients to find work. In the end even Clinton was able to say, notes historian Robert Remini, that "the era of big government is over." This announcement may have won the support of the nation's conservative element, but old-line, liberal Democrats considered Clinton a traitor to the party's traditional heritage.

THE ELECTION OF 1996

Feeling that Clinton might be vulnerable in 1996, the Republicans chose Kansas Senator Robert Dole as their candidate. A World War II veteran who had suffered a wound by which he lost the use of his right arm, Dole often held a pen in his right hand to indicate that he could not shake hands with that arm. The witty Dole ran a lackluster campaign that did not generate much enthusiasm.

During the campaign, a number of congressional investigators revealed that the president had received campaign contributions from questionable sources, including foreigners who were restricted from contributing to American candidates, and those who had given to Clinton's reelection only to be "rewarded" with an overnight stay at the White House. Yet Clinton, who had already proven himself as a masterful campaigner, repeated his 1992 victory, helped by a reviving economy. His 47 million votes outweighed Dole's 39.1 million. The electoral vote outcome was almost a mirror reflection of Clinton's first election—a massive 379 to 159. With the reelection of Clinton and the rejection of Dole, America had lost its last opportunity to elect a World War II veteran. Former vets had included the likes of Eisenhower, JFK, LBJ, Nixon, and Bush, but any future WWII vet would simply have to be considered too old.

No Democratic president had been reelected since Franklin Delano Roosevelt, yet Clinton opened his second term with a muted voice. He was no longer making far-reaching promises or vowing to retool the social landscape. Facing Republican majorities in both houses of Congress, he tended to keep his legislative goals to a minimum, as he continued his shift away from the left and back toward the center. Clinton was undoubtedly popular in America when 1997 opened, as the economy turned rosy, causing federal monies to pour in and creating budget surpluses for the first time in 30 years. That economy carried Clinton through several rough years of his second term, all the way to 2000, and represented one of the most vibrant, expanding economies in U.S. history, better by several measures than the golden era of the 1950s and early 1960s.

Yet the president found himself surrounded by controversy over his trade policies. His support of NAFTA and its aftermath still did not sit well with some Americans. Now his role in establishing the World Trade Organization (WTO), the inheritor of the older General Agreement on Tariffs and Trade (GATT), brought new rounds of protest, this time from street protesters who marched in Seattle during a 1999 meeting of the WTO. Those opposed to the organization were rallying against economic "globalization." The Seattle meeting ended in failure, and Clinton received much of the blame.

CLINTON'S FOREIGN POLICY

Clinton always was much more certain of himself on domestic issues, rather than foreign policy. His 1993 dispatch of U.S. troops to rebel-dominated Somalia for humanitarian purposes blew up on him when the rebels, led by little more than drug lords, engaged U.S. military forces in the streets of Mogadishu and killed more than a dozen soldiers. In the spring of 1994 Clinton quietly withdrew U.S. forces, having accomplished little.

Clinton took significant steps diplomatically and economically in dealing with the Chinese, including the passage of a very controversial trade bill that gave most-favored trade status to China in 2000. The step struck some Americans as ironic, as Clinton had chastised President Bush during the 1992 campaign for failing to place economic punishments on China over the Communist-led nation's human rights abuses.

Similarly, the president showed fairly indecisive leadership over the ethnic violence that was taking place in Southeastern Europe during his first term. He eventually committed U.S. troops to a NATO peacekeeping force in 1995, which helped limit violence between Christians and Muslims in Bosnia. In 1999, when Serbian President Slobodan Milosevic returned to "ethnic cleansing" by targeting ethnic Albanians in Kosovo, U.S. forces and NATO troops launched an air campaign against Serbia. In time Milosevic agreed to a NATO force to be placed in Kosovo. By 2001 the Serbian leader had been condemned as a war criminal, arrested, and tried in the International Criminal Court in The Hague. He died in 2006 before his trial was finished.

Upset in the Middle East

Clinton also struggled with various problems in the Middle East, as more than a half dozen presidents since World War II had done. In 1993, in the manner of President Carter, Clinton hosted a meeting in the White House between the leader of Israel, Yitzhak Rabin, and Yasir Arafat, the leader of the Palestine Liberation Organization (PLO), which earlier U.S. presidents had treated as a terrorist group. There the two leaders agreed in principle to self-rule for all Palestinians living in Israel. But the agreement did not bear immediate fruit, and when Rabin was assassinated two years later, Clinton and his secretary of state, Madeleine Albright, were left to struggle to repair the agreement for the remainder of his presidency. When Arafat himself died in 2004, little had been accomplished to settle the basic issues between Israelis and Palestinians. Generally, Clinton, through both his terms of office, never created a well-defined foreign policy approach, leaving him with a spotty diplomatic legacy.

POLITICS AND IMPEACHMENT

While Clinton typically remained a popular president, receiving reasonably high approval ratings fairly consistently through his two terms, scandal seemed to dog him at every turn. As early as the 1992 campaign, allegations of marital infidelity and questionable financial dealings were pointed at him from every direction. One female accuser had been a state employee, Paula Jones, who claimed that Clinton had sexually harassed her. Other accusations involved a 1978 investment by the Clintons in a resort development in Arkansas, called Whitewater. The project proved a money loser from day one. Whitewater's promoter, James McDougal— a Clinton family friend—may have illegally used monies from a savings and loan he headed to prop up the project, while using additional S&L funds to illegally contribute to Clinton's campaign fund. Although the facts were never completely clear, and the Clintons were never indicted, the scandal hung over the president like a dark cloud.

The Monica Lewinsky Scandal

The most damaging scandal involving Clinton's sexual activities involved a White House intern named Monica Lewinsky. The brewing scandal led Attorney General Janet Reno to appoint a special prosecutor, Pepperdine University Law School Professor Kenneth Starr, to investigate. Before a grand jury the president swore that he had not had sexual relations with Lewinsky. However, Lewinsky eventually admitted that she and the president had engaged in such activities, including in the Oval Office, and she produced damaging evidence to prove it.

In mid-August 1998 Clinton went on television and admitted his affair with Lewinsky, while also stating he had done nothing illegal. But the president had perjured himself under oath, and Starr believed that might "constitute grounds for impeachment." On October 8 the House adopted a resolution, by a vote of 258 to 176, instructing the Judiciary Committee to determine whether Clinton should be impeached. On December 12 the Committee agreed that the president had "committed perjury and obstructed justice," and added "it would be a dereliction of duty if we didn't proceed . . . with impeachment." On January 6, 1999, by a vote of 228 to 206, the House impeached Clinton on the perjury charge and on the obstruction of justice charge, by 221 to 212. For the first time in over 130 years and only the second time ever, a U.S. president had been impeached.

But many Americans did not support Clinton's removal from office. They had decided that the Republicans were pushing for impeachment for political reasons and actually voted several Republican House members out in the November mid-term elections. When the subsequent trial began on January 7, 1999, it was clear that not even all Republicans would vote to remove Clinton from office. After five weeks of testimony and debate the Senate voted against removal and acquitted Clinton, with 10 Republicans and all 45 Democrats voting not guilty on the perjury charge, while 50 senators voted not guilty on the second charge. (Under the Constitution, conviction required a two-thirds vote.) While the president had managed to survive removal from office, his administration emerged badly damaged and his reputation sorely tarnished.

8
Bush and Obama

The Clinton–Lewinsky scandal had stirred up bitter politics between the two parties, animosities that continued into the 2000 presidential election season. The Republicans nominated Texas Governor George Walker Bush, eldest son of former president George H.W. Bush. Dick Cheney, who had served as the elder Bush's secretary of defense, was tapped as his vice presidential running mate. The Democrats selected a ticket of Clinton's vice president Al Gore, and Connecticut Senator Joseph Lieberman.

THE 2000 CAMPAIGN

Bush campaigned as a Washington outsider, claiming that he would emphasize bipartisanship as a "uniter," not a "divider." Gore tried to put political distance between himself and Clinton, due to the scandals, but this strategy meant he could hardly claim significant credit for much that the administration had accomplished either.

The outcome of the 2000 presidential election was to prove one of the most controversial in the history of the United States. The vote was neck-and-neck. When it was announced that Bush had won the critical state of Florida, Gore conceded soon after the polls closed, certain that he would not receive enough electoral votes to win. An hour later Gore withdrew his concession: the count in Florida was in dispute.

Over the following five weeks Americans held their breath as controversy swirled over malfunctioning voting machines in Florida. Finally the U.S. Supreme Court intervened, and Florida went to Bush. (Officially, he won the state by just 537 votes out of the total 6 million cast.) This gave Bush an electoral vote victory of 271 to Gore's 266, since 270 had been the number needed to win. However, Gore had received a half million more popular votes—50.999 million to Bush's 50.456 million. Amid loud, bitter cries of political foul, Bush became the first president to win fewer popular votes than his opponent since 1888.

"BUSH 43"

For the second time in U.S. history, the son of a U.S. president had gained the White House. (John Adams and son John Quincy had been the first father-son presidential duo.) To distinguish between the two Bush presidents, people referred to them as Bush 41 and Bush 43, as they had been the 41st and 43rd presidents. As a younger man, Bush had struggled to find his own personal identity separate from his father, which had led him through years of rebelliousness. But, as a married adult with children, Bush had straightened out and had a "born again" experience under the mentorship of a popular evangelist, the Reverend Billy Graham. Bush entered the White House with political leanings that probably fell to the right of his father. He had chosen the conservative Cheney as his veep, and also surrounded himself with other powerful conservatives.

Given his conservativism, as well as his Christian beliefs, President Bush pushed for a "faith-based initiative" that would provide federal dollars for programs sponsored by religious groups. He opposed federal funding for abortion and stem-cell research. As a pro-business leader, he refused to sign the United States on as a supporter of the Kyoto Treaty, an international agreement that called for limits on greenhouse gas emissions, claiming the treaty placed restrictions on western industrialized nations, but not on growing economic powers such as India or China. Bush also favored drilling for oil in Alaska's Arctic National Wildlife Refuge, but oil exploration there made little progress during his years in office. Bush was a supporter of tax cuts and pushed for $1.3 trillion in cuts, which soon led to higher deficits. By 2004 the deficit had reached $400 billion.

TERROR AT HOME

Bush had only been president for eight months when the United States experienced the deadliest terror attack in its history. On September 11, 2001, a balmy Tuesday morning across most of the country, Islamic terrorists hijacked four planes filled with passengers, crashing two of them into the World Trade Center's Twin Towers in New York City, and one into the Pentagon in Washington. The fourth plane, likely headed for the White House or the Capitol, was brought down in a field in Pennsylvania after passengers rushed the Arab gunmen. The jets that hit the Twin Towers ignited into two balls of flame, ultimately causing the towers to completely collapse, a scene captured by news media around the world, and causing the deaths of nearly 3,000 people. Almost 250 additional people died, including the passengers and crewmembers on the hijacked airliners.

Hijacked United Airlines Flight 175 from Boston crashes into the south tower of the World Trade Center and explodes at 9:03 A.M. on September 11, 2001, in New York City. The crash of two airliners and subsequent collapse of the Twin Towers killed more than 3,000 people.

The hijackings had been planned by a radical Islamic organization called Al Qaeda, led by Osama bin Laden. Al Qaeda had backing from the Taliban leaders in Afghanistan, who had seized the government there in 1996. U.S. support for Israel and the Muslim fundamentalist belief that America represented "the great Satan"—a claim that had been leveled by Muslim extremists in 1979 during the abduction of Americans at the U.S. embassy in Tehran—were the general motivators for these wanton attacks on largely civilian populations.

War Against Afghanistan and Iraq

In the aftermath of the attacks, Americans received support and sympathy from around the world. Even the liberal French newspaper, *Le Monde*, editorialized: *"Nous sommes tous Americains"* ("We are all Americans").

Bush soon took decisive steps, calling for the destruction of Al Qaeda and the capture of Osama bin Laden—either dead or alive. Congress then passed an open-ended resolution, granting Bush authority to take any steps against "those nations, organizations, or persons he determines planned, authorized, committed, or aided the terrorist attacks that occurred on September 11, 2001." Subsequently the president ordered troops to Afghanistan to bring down the Taliban regime and to hit hard against Al Qaeda operations located in the remote Afghan frontier regions. Bin Laden managed to escape, along with many Al Qaeda members. The Taliban was pushed out of power within six months, an interim democracy was established, and a president— Hamid Karzai—elected. Yet the fight against the Taliban in the Afghan hinterland continued through both of Bush's two terms of office and beyond.

In the meantime Bush targeted the leader of Iraq, Saddam Hussein, against whom his father had gone to war 10 years earlier. Publicly, Bush justified invading Iraq by identifying Saddam's regime, along with Iran and North Korea, as part of an "axis of evil, aiming to threaten the peace of the world." Various intelligence services around the world, including the CIA, reported that Iraq was actively developing chemical, biological, or nuclear weapons of mass destruction, or WMDs. In 2003 Bush launched a U.S. military invasion of 150,000 troops into Iraq, with assistance from a handful of other nations, including Great Britain.

That war would become an albatross around Bush's neck. While U.S. forces easily made their way to Baghdad and soon facilitated its fall, along with the capture of Saddam Hussein in December 2003, Bush was unable to bring about a complete resolution to the conflict. By the end of his second term, the war in Iraq had become unpopular with a significant number of Americans, many of whom were skeptical about whether Saddam had ever been harboring WMDs in the first place.

DOMESTIC ISSUES

At home Bush pursued additional agendas in response to the 9-11 attacks. He pushed the USA Patriot Act through Congress in October 2001, which allowed the federal government to carry out extensive telephone and computer surveillance and authorized the deportation of immigrants suspected of terror activities. The act was augmented in 2003. Some Americans were uncomfortable with these acts, since they permitted the administration to wiretap citizens without having to first secure a court order.

Bush also created a cabinet-level department, Homeland Security, to coordinate the efforts of the various agencies responsible for U.S. security, including immigration, naturalization, customs, the secret service, the coast guard, and the Federal Emergency Management Act (FEMA). Including FEMA was soon seen as a mistake. When the devastating Hurricane Katrina hit the Gulf Coast, including New Orleans on August 29, 2005, FEMA stumbled badly in its attempts to alleviate the pain and suffering of hurricane victims. The hurricane, and especially the subsequent flooding, had destroyed 80 percent of New Orleans, caused 1,300 deaths, and cost $150 billion in property damages and later repairs. Another controversial move was Bush's policy of placing captured Taliban fighters from Afghanistan in detention at the U.S. military base in Guantanamo, Cuba. By doing so, the president placed those captured in something of a legal limbo. Americans were sharply divided by such detentions, but the policy remained in place through Bush's years in office.

Without question, Bush's war on terror brought much criticism and controversy, not only at home, but around the world. Even before he launched his invasion against Iraq, 10 million people in 60 countries demonstrated in February 2002 against the military action. Much of the worldwide sympathy demonstrated in the days immediately following the attacks on 9-11 had faded quickly. By the spring of 2008, 4,000 U.S. military personnel had been killed in Iraq, and thousands more had been wounded—more deaths than had been caused by the terror attacks of 9-11.

THE 2004 ELECTION

With the approach of the 2004 election the Democrats found themselves in an awkward position. They could not campaign against the war without risking appearing unsupportive or unpatriotic. Senator John Kerry of Massachusetts, who had a strong political record and had fought in the Vietnam War, gained the Democrat nomination and selected Senator John Edwards from North Carolina as his running mate. Kerry and Edwards campaigned against the Bush tax cuts and the war in Iraq, and in favor of better healthcare and more funding for education.

Bush simply ran on a platform that called for staying the course in Iraq and in the war against terror. He also favored a constitutional amendment banning same-sex marriage, a hot issue during the campaign and in subsequent years. The president's position mirrored that of many American

REBUILDING AND MEMORIALIZING

For many Americans, memories of the Islamic terrorist attacks on September 11, 2001, feature not only the vivid images of the collapse of the Twin Towers in New York, but of the piles of debris left from their fall, which included twisted heaps of metal and concrete. The cleanup of the site that came to be known as "Ground Zero" took many months, but plans were soon underway to rebuild.

Already the adjacent 7 World Trade Center has a completed office tower, finished in 2006. At 1 World Trade Center, construction is underway. The planned building will stand 1,776 feet (541 m) high, making it one of the tallest buildings in North America. Three additional towers are planned at the site near the original Twin Towers, but the downturn in the nation's economy in

2008 led to delays in the target date for completion of the project. As for the Pentagon, another terrorist target that day, the damaged portion of the military complex was reconstructed and occupied less than a year after the attack. Renovations included a private chapel and memorial where Flight 77 struck the building that fateful day. Plans were soon made for the construction of a memorial outside Shanksville, Pennsylvania, at the site where Flight 93 crashed. The Flight 93 National Memorial was scheduled to include a grove of trees marking the site, and wind chimes etched with the names of the flight's victims. The site is today marked by a cross, fashioned out of steel from the wreckage of the World Trade Center and erected by New York City firefighters.

citizens, as 11 states passed laws banning marriages between two men or two women.

Bush was reelected, taking 51 percent of the popular vote to Kerry's 48 percent, as well as the necessary number of electoral votes—279 to 252. The race was close: If Ohio, a keenly contested state, had voted for Kerry, he would have gained enough electoral votes to win. But that trend would have to wait until the 2008 election.

A SECOND TERM

Bush's second term was dominated by his war on terror, but he did have a domestic agenda as well. He sought further reductions in taxes and tried to reform Medicare. He tried to privatize much of Social Security, but abandoned the fight when he was met with furious protests. The president also fought for immigration reform, but parted ways with many conservatives by opposing the arrest and deportation of 12 million illegal aliens, most of whom were Hispanics. He proposed a guest-worker program and a process to clear the way for citizenship for undocumented workers. This plan was rejected by Congress in the summer of 2007.

As during other recent presidential second terms, the Bush administration had to handle several scandals, including the revelation that the federal government had been conducting illegal wiretapping of U.S. citizens with alleged connections to terror groups. Less than two years later the Bush Justice Department was under scrutiny over the firing of eight U.S. attorneys, allegedly for political reasons.

But, without question, it was the state of the Iraq War that most concerned the Americans who voted in the 2008 election. The war had continued for four years and the majority of people felt that opening the conflict in the first place had been a mistake. Many now believed that the fight against insurgents in Iraq was not winnable. The primary question for many no longer centered on how or why the United States had entered the conflict, but on what strategy should be pursued to remove U.S. military forces from Iraq.

A HISTORIC ELECTION

With Bush having achieved historically low popularity poll numbers, the Democrats now saw an opportunity. Several candidates entered the field, including former First Lady Hillary Rodham Clinton. She took the early lead in the campaign primaries, impressing voters with her impressive command of policy issues and backed by a campaign fund with deep pockets. Her candidacy represented the first serious female candidate for the presidency in American history. She had the support of those Americans, especially women, who were anxious for female leadership in the White House. However, it was a 46-year-old first-term senator from Chicago, Barack Obama, who finally won the Democrat nomination. An African American whose white mother was from Kansas and whose black father was from Kenya, Obama had captivated his party at its 2004 convention and had continued to shine over the next four years.

The Republican nomination went to Arizona Senator John McCain, a trusted Republican voice in the Senate, respected on both sides of the aisle, and a man of significant political experience. To make the ticket more agreeable to party conservatives, the Arizona senator surprised many when he chose Alaskan Governor Sarah Palin as his running mate, even though she had only served for 21 months and had no other political experience of note.

The 2008 election was now set to bring extraordinary results, no matter who won. A Democrat win would result in the election of the nation's first black president, while a Republican victory would place a woman in the second-highest office in the land. For many Americans, this election represented something so unique and exciting that significant numbers of people who had never really plugged into a presidential campaign season before now found themselves passionately connected.

During the campaign the attention of many Americans was drawn away from the election as the nation experienced the beginnings of an economic meltdown, starting with the bursting of the U.S. housing bubble. Beginning in September 2008 the economy seemed to implode, as the media reported waves of housing foreclosures, followed by bank collapses, and a stock market that was sliding downward at a precipitous rate. The problem was worldwide. Financial institutions from Tokyo to New York and London to Paris began to decline, as credit disappeared and stock values plummeted. Comparisons to the early days of the Great Depression were on the lips of every news pundit across the country.

With renewed concerns, and feeling as though the Bush administration was at least partially responsible for this financial collapse, voters showed up at the polls in droves to cast their ballots for Barack Obama. He took 53 percent of the popular vote, as well as 364 electoral votes to McCain's 175. States that had voted in 2004 for Bush had now gone the way of the Democrats. The party also gained significant increases in both Senate and House seats. History had been made, as the nation elected the first non-white chief executive in the history of the U.S. republic.

A SINKING ECONOMY

In the months between Obama's election and his inauguration, the U.S. economy continued to slide downward at an appalling rate. The Bush administration took emergency steps to try to place some sort of tourniquet on the problem as financial houses collapsed and stock market prices took a nosedive. The Treasury Department and Federal Reserve

System nationalized the country's two largest mortgage companies, Fannie Mae and Freddie Mac, and took control of the nation's largest private insurance company, AIG. Congress was then called by Treasury Secretary Henry Paulson to pony up $700 billion to cover the banks' risks on "toxic" mortgages. These were mortgages given during the previous

Supporters of U.S. Senator Barack Obama celebrate as his victory in the presidential election is announced in Birmingham, Alabama, on the night of November 4, 2008.

decade to individuals who did not have the means to afford them. These federal dollars were intended to inject cash into the banking system.

By the time Barack Obama was inaugurated in January 2009, the economic situation had reached the point of absolute crisis. Credit was unavailable, business and industry were closing their doors, U.S. auto companies were on the verge of bankruptcy, banks were closing, and workers were losing their jobs. During his first "100 Days" as president, Obama took serious steps of his own to fight the economy declines that were strapping the nation. He moved quickly, pushing legislation through Congress that he signed on February 17, to authorize emergency monies of nearly $800 billion. This infusion of cash to stimulate the economy was to be spent on healthcare, infrastructure, education, and direct assistance to individuals and such ailing companies as General Motors and Chrysler. With these monies, Obama promised that he would create millions of jobs. As part of his 2010 budget, Obama proposed between $2 and $3 trillion dollars for the government to spend to further stabilize the economy. Independent government officials warned that such spending would produce nearly $10 trillion in deficits over the next decade.

A Range of Policies and Changes

On other fronts, the new president took some bold steps, some of which proved controversial. Within 24 hours of his inauguration, he announced his intention to close down the detention facility at Guantanamo. By the end of 2009, the Cuban facility had not yet been closed, even as Obama chose to have accused terrorist mastermind Khalid Sheikh Mohammed tried in New York City. He also announced a timetable for the withdrawal of U.S. troops from Iraq. Obama turned around an executive order of President Bush's in order to allow federal dollars to be spent on stem cell research. He authorized some benefits for same-sex partners of federal employees. He also overturned another Bush policy and closed a five-year open window for offshore drilling for oil and natural gas in U.S. coastal waters. In May 2009, he nominated Sonia Sotomayor to the U.S. Supreme Court. With little controversy, she was approved for the Court by August, becoming the third woman and the first Latino to serve on the highest court in the land.

Tackling Healthcare

Early on in his administration President Obama called for sweeping policy changes in healthcare reform, which he had campaigned on in 2008. By July 4, 2009, House Democrats had produced and introduced a 1,000-page plan for overhauling the nation's healthcare system. Obama immediately put this on the fast track, looking for passage before the Congress's August recess. When the specifics of the bill became known, along with word that the proposed healthcare plan would add $1 trillion to the deficit during its first 10 years, Americans began to protest. They showed up at meetings around the country during the late summer weeks, with many speaking out against what was being called "Obama Care." Between his inauguration and September 2009 Obama's approval rating fell from 82 percent to 53 percent. At the end of 2009, the unemployment rate still hovered near 10 percent. Many Americans were concerned about, or actually disapproved of, his handling of the economy, his massive healthcare plan, his tax increases, the rising federal deficit, and even his handling of foreign affairs, including the fight against terror and his strategies in Afghanistan. Even when Obama announced in December 2009 that he was sending 30,000 more U.S. troops to Afghanistan, he was criticized for placing a 2011 deadline to begin withdrawal. As 2010 opened, there was little sign of change and certainly none of improvement. On the international front, relations with China soured and at home Obama's firm hand with bankers and financiers sent repercussions way beyond Wall Street. By February, with the election of Republican Scott Brown to fill Massachusetts Democrat Teddy Kennedy's former Senate seat, the Democrats lost their "super majority" of 60 votes, placing the future of a substantive health care bill in jeopardy.

AMERICA'S NEW CENTURY

As the United States finished its first decade of the twenty-first century, many Americans found themselves living in an era of uncertainty, one marked by long-standing military action abroad, a continuing and complex "war on terror," political rancor at home, and an economy that seemed to teeter on the brink of complete collapse. Yet the American spirit continues to pump new vitality, new ideas, and a new sense of idealism against these looming problems. With the elimination of such earlier challenges as the threat of Communism and the Cold War, Americans will hopefully continue to find strength in those values and ideals that have served them and their ancestors well for more than two centuries. What the future of America will be is anyone's guess. But throughout the history of the U.S. republic, the people of the United States have relied on the dreams of others who came before them; those who saw purpose in liberty, held passion for democratic thinking, and believed that tomorrow, in America, always has the potential for a brighter day.

Chronology

1964

July President Lyndon B. Johnson signs the Civil Rights Act

August Gulf of Tonkin Incident leads to Congress passing a resolution giving Johnson all necessary power to prevent aggression in Southeast Asia

November Johnson defeats Arizona Senator Barry Goldwater in the presidential election

TIMELINE

January, 1986
Space shuttle Challenger explodes after lift-off, killing all seven crew members

November, 1964
Johnson elected president

November, 1968
Nixon is elected president

May, 1970
Four students are killed by National Guardsmen during a protest at Kent State (IN.) University

November, 1984
Reagan reelected as president

November, 1980
Reagan is elected president

| 1964 | 1970 | 1975 | 1980 | 1987 |

April, 1968
Dr. Martin Luther King is assassinated in Memphis

June, 1968
Senator Robert Kennedy assassinated in Los Angeles

August, 1974
Nixon resigns his office

August, 1974
Ford becomes president

July, 1969
U.S. astronauts land on the moon

November, 1976
Carter is elected president

June, 1987
Reagan delivers "Tear Down This Wall" speech in Berlin

1965

February Viet Cong attack on U.S. military base at Pleiku kills eight marines. Days following, Johnson approves ground troops in Vietnam

August Johnson signs the Voting Rights Act

1967 Antiwar movement gains traction across the country

1968

January North Vietnamese launch Tet Offensive

March Johnson's Secretary of Defense, Robert McNamara, resigns from office

April Dr. Martin Luther King Jr. is assassinated in Memphis

November, 2000
George W. Bush defeats Al Gore in a close presidential race

September, 2001
Arab terrorists fly planes into World Trade Center towers and the Pentagon

January, 1991
The Persian Gulf War opens

November, 2008
Obama elected president

November, 1992
Clinton defeats Bush in presidential election

March, 2003
Bush invades Iraq

1988   **1995**   **2000**   **2005**   **2010**

April, 1999
School shooting at Columbine High School leaves 15 dead

September, 2005
Hurricane Katrina devastates the Gulf Coast region

January, 2009 President Obama authorizes emergency monies of $800 billion to ease the serious crisis in the economy

November, 1988
George H. W. Bush defeats Dukakis in presidential election

December, 2009
The United States sends 30,000 more troops to Afghanistan to fight the Taliban

June Senator Robert Kennedy is assassinated in Los
   Angeles

November Richard Nixon is elected president, defeating
   Hubert Humphrey

1969

July U.S. astronauts land on the Moon

August Woodstock Music Festival is held in upstate New York

1970

May Four students are killed by National Guardsmen
   during a protest at Kent State University

1971

July Twenty-sixth Amendment to the Constitution is
   ratified, lowering the voting age from 21 to 18

1972

February President Nixon visits Communist China

May American and Soviet officials sign SALT I

June The Watergate burglars are arrested

October National Security Adviser Henry Kissinger
   announces that peace agreement over Vietnam is
   close at hand

November Nixon defeats McGovern to win second
   term as president

1973

January The Supreme Court decision *Roe v. Wade*
   legalizes abortion in America. The Vietnam War
   ceasefire comes into effect

March Last American troops leave South Vietnam

April White House advisers H. R. Haldeman, John
   Ehrlichman, and John Dean resign their posts

October Vice President Spiro Agnew resigns his office.
   U.S. influence brings an end to the Six Day War in
   Middle East between Israel and Egypt

December Gerald Ford is sworn in as Nixon's next vice
   president

1974

April Nixon releases full transcripts of the White House tapes

July House Judiciary Committee recommends that Nixon should be impeached

August Nixon resigns his office

September Ford pardons Nixon

1976

July The nation celebrates the 200th anniversary of the adoption of the Declaration of Independence

November Jimmy Carter is elected president

1977

September Carter signs treaty to turn control of the Panama Canal over to Panama by 1999

1978

September Carter meets with Egyptian President Anwar Sadat and Israeli Prime Minister Menachem Begin at Camp David

1979

January United States establishes diplomatic ties with Communist China for first time since 1949

March The nuclear reactor at Three Mile Island outside Harrisburg, Pennsylvania, malfunctions

November Iranian students storm the U.S. embassy in Tehran and take American hostages

1980

April A U.S. mission to rescue hostages in Iran is aborted after accidental deaths of eight servicemen

November Ronald Reagan is elected president

1981

January The U.S. hostages are freed in Tehran

March President Reagan is shot by mentally disturbed young man but soon recovers

September Sandra Day O'Connor is sworn in as the first woman Supreme Court justice

1983

March Reagan announces U.S. Strategic Defence Initiative (SDI) or "Star Wars" plan

1984

November Reagan defeats Mondale and gains a second term

1985

July United States makes secret arms sale to Iran, resulting in release of one of seven known hostages

November Reagan and the new leader of the Soviet Union, Mikhail Gorbachev, meet in Geneva, Switzerland, for a summit

1986

January Space shuttle *Challenger* explodes after lift-off, killing all seven crew members

May United States makes second secret arms sale to Iran

November The Iran–Contra Scandal breaks

1987

June Reagan delivers "Tear Down This Wall" speech in Berlin

October Stock market crashes

November Reagan and Gorbachev agree on the Intermediate-range Nuclear Forces (INF) Treaty

1988

November George Herbert Walker Bush defeats Michael Dukakis in the presidential election

1989

November The Berlin Wall falls

December U.S. troops invade Panama to capture General Manuel Noriega

1990

July Congress passes Americans with Disabilities Act

August Iraqi forces invade neighboring Kuwait

October East and West Germany are reunified

1991

January The Persian Gulf War opens

1992

February Bush and Yeltsin meet at Camp David and formally declare an end to the Cold War

November Bill Clinton defeats George H. W. Bush in presidential election

1993

February A terrorist bomb explodes in the basement garage of World Trade Center

April The Branch Davidian compound outside Waco is scene of standoff with federal agents

October 18 U.S. soldiers are killed by Somalis in Mogadishu

December Clinton signs the North American Free Trade Agreement (NAFTA)

1994

May Paula Jones files a federal lawsuit against President Clinton for sexual harassment

1995

April Bombing of a federal office building in Oklahoma City kills 168

August Clinton commits U.S. troops to a NATO peacekeeping force in order to limit violence between Christians and Muslims in Bosnia

1996

November Clinton is elected to a second term, defeating Bob Dole

1998

January Clinton denies on television having had an affair with Monica Lewinsky

August Clinton admits on television having had an affair with Monica Lewinsky

December House of Representatives votes to impeach Clinton

1999

February Senate acquits Clinton of impeachment charges

April Shooting at Columbine High School leaves 15 dead

2000

> *November* George Walker Bush defeats Al Gore in a close presidential race

2001

> *September* Arab terrorists fly planes into World Trade Center towers and the Pentagon
>
> *December* Bush sends troops to Afghanistan to topple Taliban

2002

> *January* Bush delivers speech referring to Iran, Iraq, and North Korea as "axis of evil"

2003

> *March* Bush invades Iraq

2005

> *September* Hurricane Katrina devastates the Gulf Coast region, including city of New Orleans

2007

> *January* Nancy Pelosi becomes first woman Speaker of the House of Representatives

2008

> *November* Barack Obama is elected the nation's first black president

2009

> *January* President Obama authorizes emergency monies of $800 billion to ease the serious crisis in the economy
>
> *July* President Obama introduces a radical plan for overhauling the healthcare system
>
> *December* The United States sends 30,000 more troops to Afghanistan to fight the Taliban

2010

> *January* Republican Scott Brown is elected senator of Massachusetts, causing the Democrats to lose their "super majority"

Glossary

Arms Race A massive military build-up, especially of nuclear weapons, by both the Soviet Union and the United States in an effort to gain military superiority.

baby boomer An American born between 1946 and 1964, during the baby boom that followed the end of World War II.

bipolar The world view that the United States and the Soviet Union represented the two political powers that had the majority of economic, military, and cultural influence internationally.

Black Power A movement that began in the mid-1960s and called for renewed racial pride for blacks in America. The movement did not support complete integration, believing that this would represent a surrender to the dominant white social order.

Branch Davidians A religious sect, led by a charismatic leader named David Koresh. Their commune near Waco, Texas was put under siege by government agents in April 1993 and eventually destroyed by fire.

Camp David Accords A historic treaty between Egypt and Israel, brokered by President Carter at Camp David in 1978, under which Egypt agreed to recognize the right of Israel to exist.

civil rights The rights of individuals to be free from unfair or unequal treatment (discrimination) based on their race, gender, religion, national origin, disability, sexual orientation, age, or other protected characteristic.

Civil Rights Movement Historically, the campaign to achieve true equality for African-Americans in all facets of society. Today the term is also used to describe the advancement of equality for all people, regardless of race, sex, age, disability, national origin, religion, sexual orientation, or other protected characteristic.

Cold War The struggle for power between the Soviet Union and the United States that lasted from the end of World War II until the collapse of the Soviet Union. The war was considered "cold" because the aggression was ideological, economic, and diplomatic rather than a direct military conflict.

Communism A political theory, according to which collective ownership of property leads to a classless society. Under the Communist government in the Soviet Union, the state owned all means of production and was led by a centralized, authoritarian party. This was viewed as the antithesis of democracy in the United States.

containment The core U.S. foreign policy during the Cold War of which the "Truman Doctrine" was an early part. The United States tried to "contain" Communism by preventing it from spreading to other countries.

"Contract With America" A Republican election platform of 1994 that promised action on such issues as a balanced budget amendment and term limits for members of Congress.

Contras A military force in Nicaragua, trained by the United States to oppose the socialist Nicaraguan government led by the Sandinista party.

desegregation The breaking down of imposed racial separation. Desegregation is a fundamental aim of the U.S. civil rights movement and was given special impetus by a 1954 Supreme Court decision.

détente An easing of tensions between countries, which usually leads to increased economic, diplomatic, and other types of contact between former rivals. The policy sometimes marked relations between the United States and the Soviet Union during the 1970s and 1980s.

discrimination The act, practice, or an instance of discriminating categorically rather than individually; a prejudiced or prejudicial outlook, action, or treatment.

Domino Theory The theory that if one nation fell under Communist control, neighboring nations would also fall.

embargo The refusal to sell goods or commodities to a nation or group of nations. During the 1970s the oil-producing nations placed an embargo on oil exports to Western nations.

Equal Rights Amendment A proposed change to the U.S. Constitution, which was designed to provide equal rights for women. The amendment passed Congress in 1972, but was never ratified.

Gulf of Tonkin Resolution A resolution passed by Congress in August 1964, which authorized President Johnson to pursue military goals for the purpose of deterring Communist aggression in Vietnam.

impeachment Charging a public official, especially a president, with misconduct in office.

Inter-Continental Ballistic Missile (ICBM) A missile that could carry a nuclear bomb across thousands of miles.

Kyoto Treaty An international agreement to limit greenhouse gas emissions that took effect in 2005. Although signed by 169 nations, including the United States, the protocol has not been ratified by the Senate on the basis that it will hamper U.S. economic growth.

National Association for the Advancement of Colored People (NAACP) One of the oldest and most influential civil rights organizations in the United States. It was founded on February 12, 1909.

9-11 (September 11, 2001) On this date Al Qaeda terrorists carried out a series of coordinated suicide attacks against the United States. They used hijacked planes to destroy the World Trade Center towers in New York and damage the Pentagon in Washington, D.C.

Nixon Doctrine President Nixon's foreign policy, which stated the United States would form alliances with nation-friends around the world, but leave the "basic responsibility" for their defense to those nations themselves.

racism A belief in the moral or biological superiority of one race or ethnic group over another or others.

Roe v. Wade A Supreme Court decision, made in 1973. Along with *Doe v. Bolton*, this decision legalized abortion in the first trimester of pregnancy.

segregation The separation or isolation of a race, class, or ethnic group, by enforced or voluntary residence in a restricted area, by barriers to social intercourse, by separate educational facilities, or by other discriminatory means.

"Silent Majority" President Nixon's term for largely middle-class Americans who supported his administration and the Vietnam War, even as detractors of the war protested in public.

Soviet Union A country that consisted of what is now Russia, Armenia, Azerbaijan, Belarus, Estonia, Georgia, Kazakhstan, Kyrgyzstan, Latvia, Lithuania, Moldova, Tajikistan, Turkmenistan, Ukraine, and Uzbekistan.

Strategic Defense Initiative (SDI) A research and development program of the U.S. government, tasked with developing a space-based system to defend the nation from attack by strategic ballistic missiles.

Students for a Democratic Society (SDS) Formed in Port Huron, Michigan, in 1962, this group became one of the leading New Left antiwar organizations of the 1960s.

superpower A country that dominates in political and military power. During the Cold War, there were two superpowers: the Soviet Union and the United States.

Supply-Side Economics An economic theory, according to which economic growth may be maximized in a capitalist system where incentives such as lowering taxes and reduced government regulation are applied. The term was coined in 1975 and President Reagan's application of the theory was often called "Reaganomics."

Tet Offensive A military operation launched by the North Vietnamese and Viet Cong in January 1968. Though beaten back ultimately, there were tremendous casualties and the scope of the offensive indicated the failures of U.S. military policy.

Viet Cong Irregular South Vietnamese combatants, who supported the Communist North Vietnamese military forces against the United States.

Vietnamization A policy developed during the Nixon years, whereby the South Vietnamese were to ultimately assume more of the military burdens of the Vietnam War. Generally, this policy was a failure.

War on Terror A term used by President George W. Bush following the 9-11 attacks to refer to America's response. This included U.S. military action in Afghanistan and Iraq, as well as other covert actions and domestic surveillance. The term was generally rejected by the Obama administration.

Watergate A scandal involving the Nixon administration, which involved the 1972 burglarizing of the Democratic National Headquarters at the Watergate complex in Washington, D.C. and the cover-up that followed. Watergate ultimately led to Nixon's resignation.

The West In the context of the Cold War, the anticommunist nations of Western Europe and North America, which joined together in formal military alliance through the North Atlantic Treaty Organization (NATO).

Bibliography

ABC News. July 5, 2009.

Ayers, Edward, et al. *American Passages: A History of the United States.* Belmont, CA: Thomson Higher Education, 2007.

Beschloss, Michael. *Presidential Courage: Brave Leaders and How They Changed America, 1789–1989.* New York: Simon & Schuster, 2007.

Fischer, Klaus P. *America in White, Black, and Gray: The Stormy 1960s.* New York: Continuum Books, 2007.

Ford, Gerald. *A Time to Heal: The Autobiography of Gerald Ford.* New York: Harper & Row, 1979.

Gaddis, John Lewis. *The Cold War: A New History.* New York: Penguin Press, 2005.

Gitlin, Todd. *The Sixties: Years of Hope, Days of Rage.* New York: Bantam Books, 1987.

Golway, Terry. *Ronald Reagan's America: His Voice, His Dreams, and His Vision of Tomorrow.* Naperville, IL: Sourcebooks MediaFusion, 2008.

Harrington, Michael. *The Other America; Poverty in the United States.* New York: Macmillan, 1964.

Karnow, Stanley. *Vietnam: A History.* New York: Penguin Books, 1991.

Kennedy, David. *The American Pageant.* Boston: Wadsworth, 2010.

Leuchtenburg, William E. *"American Profile: Jimmy Carter."* In Allen Weinstein's *The Story of America.* New York: DK Publishing Company, 2002.

Montefiore, Simon Sebag. *Speeches That Changed the World.* London: Quercus Publishing Ltd., 2005.

Patterson, James. *Restless Giant: The United States From Watergate to Bush v. Gore.* New York: Oxford University Press, 2005.

Reagan, Ronald. *An American Life.* New York: Pocket Books, 1999.

Remini, Robert. *A Short History of the United States.* New York: HarperCollins, 2008.

Smith, Carter. *Presidents: Every Question Answered.* New York: Metro Books, 2008.

Tindall, George. *America: A Narrative History.* New York: W. W. Norton & Company, 1997.

Unger, Irwin, and Debi Unger. *America in the 1960s.* St. James, NY: Brandywine Press, 1988.

Weinstein, Allen. *The Story of America: Freedom and Crisis From Settlement to Superpower.* New York: DK Publishing, Inc., 2002.

Wolfe, Tom. *In Our Time.* New York: Farrar, Straus, & Giroux, 1980.

Further Resources

Benson, Michael. *Bill Clinton*. Minneapolis: Lerner Publishing Group, 2003.

Carlisle, Rodney P. *Persian Gulf War*. New York: Facts on File, Inc., 2003.

Donaldson, Madeline. *Richard M. Nixon*. Minneapolis: Lerner Publishing Group, 2008.

Edelman, Rob. *Watergate*. Farmington Hills, MI: Cengage Gale, 2005.

Edwards, Roberta. *Barack Obama: An American Story*. New York: Penguin Group (USA), 2009.

Englar, Mary. *September 11*. Mankato, MN: Coughlan Publishing, 2006.

Feinstein, Stephen. *Barack Obama*. Berkeley Heights, NJ: Enslow Publishers, Inc., 2008.

Gunderson, Megan M. *Lyndon B. Johnson*. Edina, MN: ABDO Publishing Company, 2009.

Hillstrom, Kevin. *Watergate*. Detroit, MI: Omnigraphics, Inc., 2004.

Joseph, Paul. *George Bush*. Edina, MN: ABDO Publishing Company, 1999.

——. *Richard Nixon*. Edina, MN: ABDO Publishing Company, 1999.

Kaufman, Burton I. *The Carter Years*. New York: Facts on File, Inc., 2006.

Levy, Debbie. *Vietnam War*. Minneapolis: Lerner Publishing Group, 2004.

Mara, Will. *George W. Bush*. New York: Scholastic Library Publishing, 2003.

Marquez, Heron. *George W. Bush*. Minneapolis: Lerner Publishing Group, 2005.

McConnell, William S. *Watergate*. Farmington Hills, MI: Cegage Gale, 2005.

McCullum, Sean. *Bill Clinton*. New York: Scholastic Library Publishing, 2005.

McNeese, Tim. *The Civil Rights Movement*. New York: Chelsea House Publishers, 2008.

———. *H. Norman Schwarzkopf*. New York: Chelsea House Publishers, 2004

Murdico, Suzanne J. *Gulf War*. New York: Rosen Publishing Group, Inc., 2004.

Pach, Chester. *The Johnson Years*. New York: Facts on File, Inc., 2005.

Schomp, Virginia. *The Vietnam War*. Tarrytown, NY: Marshall Cavendish, Inc., 2001.

Schraff, Anne. *Jimmy Carter*. Berkeley Heights, NJ: Enslow Publishers, Inc., 1998.

Stein, Conrad. *Gerald R. Ford*. New York: Scholastic Library Publishing, 2005.

Waxman, Laura Hamilton. *Gerald R. Ford*. Minneapolis: Lerner Classroom, 2007.

Williams, Jean Kinney. *Lyndon B. Johnson*. New York: Scholastic Library Publishing, 2005.

Web sites

President Lyndon Johnson:
  http://www.whitehouse.gov/about/presidents/LyndonJohnson/
  http://www.lbjlib.utexas.edu/johnson/archives.hom/
      biographys.hom/lbj_bio.asp

Vietnam War:
  http://www.pbs.org/battlefieldvietnam/
  http://www.historyplace.com/unitedstates/vietnam/index.html
  http://www.youtube.com/watch?v=sL7N-aCtlLo
      (Footage of Vietnam War)
  http://www.youtube.com/watch?v=IC4tpeN6pj4
      (Footage of Vietnam War)

Further Resources

Civil Rights Movement:
   http://www.africanaonline.com/civil_rights.htm
   http://www.martinlutherking.org/
   http://www.youtube.com/watch?v=o0FiCxZKuv8
        (Martin Luther King's last speech)
   http://www.youtube.com/watch?v=cmOBbxgxKvo
        (CBS broadcast announcing death of Martin Luther King)

Richard Nixon:
   http://www.nixonlibraryfoundation.org/
   http://www.youtube.com/watch?v=ZEOGJJ7UKFM
        (Video of Nixon resigning presidency)
   http://watergate.info/

Counterculture:
   http://www.youtube.com/watch?v=TJ4QF45Vygw
        (Footage of Woodstock)
   http://www.youtube.com/watch?v=_PFCgAhZEO8
        (Footage of Woodstock)
   http://www.youtube.com/watch?v=6jYT1p-M8P8
        (Footage of Hippies in San Francisco's "Summer of Love,
        1967")

Gerald Ford:
   http://www.fordlibrarymuseum.gov/

Jimmy Carter:
   http://www.jimmycarterlibrary.gov/

Picture Credits

Index

About the Author

Tim McNeese is associate professor of history at York College in York, Nebraska. Professor McNeese holds degrees from York College, Harding University, and Missouri State University. He has published more than 100 books and educational materials. His writing has earned him a citation in the library reference work, *Contemporary Authors* and multiple citations in *Best Books for Young Teen Readers*. In 2006, Tim appeared on the History Channel program, *Risk Takers, History Makers: John Wesley Powell and the Grand Canyon*. He was been a faculty member at the Tony Hillerman Writers Conference in Albuquerque. His wife, Beverly, is assistant professor of English at York College. They have two married children, Noah and Summer, and four grandchildren—Ethan, Adrianna, Finn William, and Beckett. Tim and Bev have sponsored college study trips on the Lewis and Clark Trail, to the American Southwest, and to New England. You may contact Professor McNeese at tdmcneese@york.edu.

About the Consultant

Richard Jensen is Research Professor at Montana State University, Billings. He has published 11 books on a wide range of topics in American political, social, military, and economic history, as well as computer methods. After taking a Ph.D. at Yale in 1966, he taught at numerous universities, including Washington, Michigan, Harvard, Illinois-Chicago, West Point, and Moscow State University in Russia.